The Lectionary
2011

First published in Great Britain in 2010

Society for Promoting Christian Knowledge
36 Causton Street
London SW1P 4ST
www.spckpublishing.co.uk

British Library Cataloguing-in-Publication Data
A catalogue record for this book is available from the British Library

ISBN 978-0-281-06340-6

1 3 5 7 9 10 8 6 4 2

Typeset by Graphicraft Ltd, Hong Kong

Printed in Great Britain by Thomson Litho

Produced on paper from sustainable forests

CONTENTS

Understanding the Lectionary   4

Making Choices in *Common Worship*   6

Book of Common Prayer   6

Certain Days and Occasions Commonly Observed   7

Key to Liturgical Colours   7

Principal Feasts, Holy Days and Festivals   8

Lesser Festivals and Commemorations   8

Lesser Festivals and Commemorations not observed in 2010–11   9

   Common Worship   9

   Book of Common Prayer   10

The Common of the Saints   11

Special Occasions   12

The *Common Worship* Calendar and Lectionary (including the
   Book of Common Prayer Calendar and Lectionary)   14

Calendar 2011   96

Calendar 2012   96

Column 1
The date

Column 3 (Common Worship)
On Principal Feasts, Principal Holy Days, Sundays and Festivals this gives the Principal Service Lectionary, intended for use at the main service of the day (in most churches the mid-morning service), whether or not it is a Eucharist.

On other weekdays this gives the Daily Eucharistic Lectionary for those wanting a semi-continuous pattern of readings and a psalm for Holy Communion. It is most useful in a church where there is a daily celebration and a core community that worships together day by day, though its use is not restricted to that.

Column 4 (Common Worship)
On Principal Feasts, Principal Holy Days, Sundays and Festivals this gives the Third Service Lectionary. Many churches will have no need of it, for it comes into use only if the Principal and Second Service Lectionaries have been used. Its most likely use is at Morning Prayer (when this is not the Principal Service). Where psalms are recommended for use in the morning, these also appear in this column.

On other weekdays this provides the psalmody and readings for Morning Prayer. Where two or more psalms are appointed, the psalm in bold italic may be used as the only psalm. Psalms printed in round brackets ( ) may be omitted if they are used as an opening canticle at Morning Prayer. Where † is printed after the psalm number; the psalm may be shortened if desired. For those wishing to follow the Ordinary Time psalm cycle throughout the year (except for the period between 19 December and the Epiphany and from the Monday of Holy Week to the Saturday of Easter Week), this is printed as an alternative to the seasonal provision.

COMMON WORSHIP

July 2011

			Sunday Principal Service Weekday Eucharist	Third Service Morning Prayer
24	S	THE FIFTH SUNDAY AFTER TRINITY **(Proper 12)**		
		Track 1	*Track 2*	
		Gen. 29. 15–28	1 Kings 3. 5–12	Ps. 77
		Ps. 105. 1–11, 45b (or 105. 1–11)	Ps. 119. 129–136	Song of Sol. ch. 2
		or Ps. 128	Rom. 8. 26–end	or 1 Macc. 2. [1–14] 15–22
		Rom. 8. 26–end	Matt. 13. 31–33, 44–52	1 Pet. 4. 7–14
		Matt. 13. 31–33, 44–52		
	G			
25 DEL 17	M	JAMES THE APOSTLE	Jer. 45. 1–5 or Acts 11.27 – 12.2 Ps. 126 Acts 11.27 – 12.2 or 2 Cor. 4. 7 –15	MP: Ps. 7; 29; 117 2 Kings 1. 9–15 Luke 9. 46–56
	R		Matt. 20. 20–28	
26	Tu	Anne and Joachim, Parents of the Blessed Virgin Mary		
		Zeph. 3. 14–18a	or Exod. 33. 7–11; 34. 5–9, 28	Ps. 106† (or 103)
		Ps. 127	Ps. 103. 8–12	Neh. 13. 1–14
		Rom. 8. 28–30	Matt. 13. 36–43	2 Cor. 1.15 – 2.4
	Gw	Matt. 13. 16–17		

Week number of Daily Eucharistic Lectionary

Column 2 provides for Common Worship:
* the name of the Principal Holy Day, Sunday, Festival or Lesser Festival;
* a note of other Commemorations for mention in prayers;
* any general note that applies to the whole *Common Worship* provision for the day;
* one of the options where there are two options for readings at the Eucharist or Principal Service;
* an indication of the liturgical colour.

Readings: Readings occur in this column only in two circumstances. On Sundays after Trinity where there are two 'tracks' for the Principal Service readings (where there is a choice of first reading and psalm, but the second reading and Gospel are the same in both tracks), Track I appears in this column. On Lesser Festivals throughout the year, where there are readings for that festival that are alternative to the semi-continuous Daily Eucharistic Lectionary, these also appear in this column.

Colour: An upper-case letter indicates the liturgical colour of the day. A lower-case second colour indicates the colour for a Lesser Festival while the upper-case letter indicates the continuing seasonal colour.

LECTIONARY

BOOK OF COMMON PRAYER

Second Service Evening Prayer	Calendar and Holy Communion	Morning Prayer	Evening Prayer
	THE FIFTH SUNDAY AFTER TRINITY		
Ps. 75; [76]	I Kings 19. 19–21	Ps. 77	Ps. 75; [76]
I Kings 6. 11–14, 23–end	Ps. 84. 8–end	Song of Sol. ch. 2	I Kings 6. 11–14, 23–end
Acts 12. 1–17	I Pet. 3. 8–15a	or I Macc. 2. [1–14]	Acts 12. 1–17
Gospel: John 6. 1–21	Luke 5. 1–11	15–22	or First EP of James
or First EP of James		I Pet. 4. 7–14	Ps. 144
Ps. 144			Deut. 30. 11–end
Deut. 30. 11–end			Mark 5. 12–end
Mark 5. 12–end			R ct
R ct	G		
	JAMES THE APOSTLE		
EP: Ps. 94	2 Kings 1. 9–15	(Ps. 7; 29; 117)	(Ps. 94)
Jer. 26. 1–15	Ps. 15	Jer. 45. 1–5	Jer. 26. 1–15
Mark 1. 14–20	Acts 11.27 – 12.3a	Luke 9. 46–56	Mark 1. 14–20
	Matt. 20. 20–28		
	R		
	Anne, Mother of the Blessed Virgin Mary		
Ps. 107†	Com. Saint	Neh. 13. 1–14	I Sam. 1.21 – 2.11
I Sam. 1.21 – 2.11		2 Cor. 1.15 – 2.4	Luke 19. 41–end
Luke 19. 41–end			
	Gw		

Making Choices in *Common Worship*

Common Worship makes provision for a variety of pastoral and liturgical circumstances. It needs to, for it has to serve some church communities where Morning Prayer, Holy Communion and Evening Prayer are all celebrated every day, and yet be useful also in a church with only one service a week, and that service varying in form and time from week to week.

At the beginning of the year, some decisions in principle need to be taken.

In relation to the Calendar, a decision needs to be taken whether to keep The Epiphany on Thursday 6 January or on Sunday 2 January, The Presentation of Christ (Candlemas) on Wednesday 2 February or on Sunday 30 January and whether to keep the Feast of All Saints on Tuesday 1 November or on Sunday 30 October.

In relation to the Lectionary, the initial choices every year to decide in relation to Sundays are:

- which of the services on a Principal Feast, Principal Holy Day, Sunday or Festival constitutes the 'Principal Service'; then use the Principal Service Lectionary (column 3) consistently for that service through the year;
- during the Sundays after Trinity, whether to use Track 1 of the Principal Service Lectionary (column 2), where the first reading stays over several weeks with one Old Testament book read semi-continuously, or Track 2 (column 3), where the first reading is chosen for its relationship to the Gospel reading of the day;
- which, if any, service on a Principal Feast, Principal Holy Day, Sunday or Festival constitutes the 'Second Service'; then use the Second Service Lectionary (column 5) consistently for that service through the year;
- which, if any, service on a Principal Feast, Principal Holy Day, Sunday or Festival constitutes the 'Third Service'; then use the Third Service Lectionary (column 4) consistently for that service through the year.

And in relation to weekdays:

- whether to use the Daily Eucharistic Lectionary (column 3) consistently for weekday celebrations of Holy Communion (with the exception of Principal Feasts, Principal Holy Days and Festivals) or to make some use of the Lesser Festival provision;
- whether to follow the first psalm provision in column 4 (morning) and column 5 (evening), where psalms during the seasons have a seasonal flavour but in ordinary time follow a sequential pattern; or to follow the alternative provision in the same columns, where psalms follow the sequential pattern throughout the year, except for the period between 19 December and The Epiphany and from the Monday of Holy Week to the Saturday of Easter Week; or to follow the psalm cycle in the Book of Common Prayer, where they are nearly always used 'in course'.

The flexibility of *Common Worship* is intended to enable the church and the minister to find the most helpful provision for them. But once a decision is made, it is advisable to stay with that decision through the year or at the very least through a complete season.

Book of Common Prayer

A separate Lectionary for the Book of Common Prayer is no longer issued. Provision is made on the right-hand pages of this Lectionary for BCP worship on all Sundays in the year, for the major festivals and for Morning and Evening Prayer. The Epistles and Gospels for Holy Communion are those of 1662, with the additions and variations of 1928, now authorized under the *Common Worship* overall provision. The Old Testament readings and psalms for these services, formerly appended to the Series One Holy Communion service, may be used but are not mandatory with the 1662 order.

Readings for Morning and Evening Prayer, which are the same as those for *Common Worship*, are set out in the BCP section for Sundays and weekdays. The special psalm provision of the BCP is given. Otherwise the Psalter is read in course daily through each month.

The Calendar observes BCP dates when these differ from those of *Common Worship*; for example, St Thomas on 21 December. Additional commemorations in the *Common Worship* Calendar are not included, but those who wish to observe them may use the *Collects and Post Communions in Traditional Language: Lesser Festivals, Common of the Saints, Special Occasions* (Church House Publishing).

The Lectionaries of 1871 and 1922, to be found in many copies of the BCP, are still authorized and may be used, but (with the exception of the psalms and readings for Holy Communion mentioned above) the Additional Alternative Lectionary (1961) is no longer authorized for public worship.

Although those who use the BCP, for private or public worship or both, are free to follow any of the authorized lectionaries, there is much to be said for common usage across the Church of England, so that the same passages are being read by all. It is of course appropriate that BCP readings should be taken from the Authorized or King James Version for harmony of style, with the daily recitation of the BCP Psalter.

The integrity of the BCP as the traditional source of worship in the Church of England is not in any way affected by the use of a common lectionary for the daily offices.

CERTAIN DAYS AND OCCASIONS COMMONLY OBSERVED

Plough Sunday may be observed on 9 January 2011.

The Week of Prayer for Christian Unity may be observed from 18 to 25 January 2011.

Education Sunday may be observed on 20 February 2011.

Rogation Sunday may be observed on 29 May 2011.

The Feast of Dedication is observed on the anniversary of the dedication or consecration of a church, or, when the actual date is unknown, on 2 October 2011. In CW, 23 October 2011 is an alternative date.

Ember Days. CW encourages the bishop to set the Ember Days in each diocese in the week before the ordinations, whereas in BCP the dates are fixed.

Days of Discipline and Self-Denial in CW are the weekdays of Lent and all Fridays in the year, except all Principal Feasts and festivals outside Lent and Fridays between Easter Day and Pentecost. The eves of Principal Feasts are also appropriately kept as days of discipline and self-denial in preparation for the feast.

Days of Fasting and Abstinence according to the BCP are the forty days of Lent, the Ember Days at the four seasons, the three Rogation Days, and all Fridays in the year except Christmas Day. The BCP also orders the observance of the Evens or Vigils before The Nativity of our Lord, The Purification of the Blessed Virgin Mary, The Annunciation of the Blessed Virgin Mary, Easter Day, Ascension Day, Pentecost, and before the following saints' days: Matthias, John the Baptist, Peter, James, Bartholomew, Matthew, Simon and Jude, Andrew, Thomas, and All Saints. (If any of these days falls on Monday, the Vigil is to be kept on the previous Saturday.)

KEY TO LITURGICAL COLOURS

Common Worship suggests appropriate liturgical colours. They are not mandatory, and traditional or local use may be followed.

For a detailed discussion of when colours may be used, see *Common Worship: Services and Prayers for the Church of England* (Church House Publishing), *New Handbook of Pastoral Liturgy* (SPCK) or *A Companion to Common Worship: Volume I* (SPCK).

W   White
𝕎   Gold or white
R   Red
P   Purple (may vary from 'Roman purple' to violet, with blue as an alternative; a Lent array of sackcloth may be used in Lent, and rose pink on The Third Sunday of Advent and Fourth Sunday of Lent)
G   Green

When a lower-case letter accompanies an upper-case letter, the lower-case letter indicates the liturgical colour appropriate to the Lesser Festival of that day, while the upper-case letter indicates the continuing seasonal colour.

PRINCIPAL FEASTS, HOLY DAYS AND FESTIVALS

Principal Feasts, and other Principal Holy Days (Ash Wednesday, Maundy Thursday, Good Friday), are printed in **LARGE BOLD CAPITALS** in the Lectionary.

There are no longer proper readings relating to the Holy Spirit on the six days after Pentecost. Instead they have been located on the nine days before Pentecost.

When Patronal and Dedication Festivals are kept as Principal Feasts, they may be transferred to the nearest Sunday, unless that day is already either a Principal Feast or The First Sunday of Advent, The Baptism of Christ, The First Sunday of Lent or Palm Sunday.

Festivals are printed in the Lectionary in SMALL BOLD CAPITALS.

For each day there is a full liturgical provision for the Holy Communion and for Morning and Evening Prayer. Most holy days that are in the category 'Festival' are provided with an optional First Evening Prayer. Its use is entirely at the discretion of the minister. Where it is used, the liturgical colour for the next day should be used at that First Evening Prayer and this has been indicated in the provision on the following pages.

LESSER FESTIVALS AND COMMEMORATIONS

Lesser Festivals (printed in **bold roman** typeface) are observed at the level appropriate to a particular church. The readings and psalms for The Common of the Saints are listed on page 11. In addition, there are special readings appropriate to the Festival listed in the first column. The daily psalms and readings at Morning and Evening Prayer are not usually superseded by those for Lesser Festivals, but the readings and psalms for Holy Communion may on occasion be used at Morning or Evening Prayer.

Commemorations are printed in the Lectionary in *italic* typeface. They do not have collect, psalm or readings, but may be observed by mention in prayers of intercession and thanksgiving. For local reasons, or where there is an established tradition in the wider Church, they may be kept as Lesser Festivals using the appropriate material from The Common of the Saints. Equally, it may be desirable to observe some Lesser Festivals as Commemorations.

If a Lesser Festival or a Commemoration falls on a Principal Feast, Principal Holy Day, Sunday or Festival, it is not normally observed that year, although it may be celebrated, where there is sufficient reason, on the nearest available day. Lesser Festivals and Commemorations which, for this reason, would not be celebrated in 2010–11 are listed on pages 9–10, so that, if desired, they may be mentioned in prayers of intercession and thanksgiving.

LESSER FESTIVALS AND COMMEMORATIONS NOT OBSERVED IN 2010–11

The Lesser Festivals and Commemorations (shown in italics) listed below fall on a Sunday or during Holy Week or Easter Week this year, and are thus not observed in this lectionary.

Common Worship

2011

January
2   Basil the Great and Gregory of Nazianzus, Bishops, Teachers, 379 and 389
     Seraphim, Monk of Sarov, Spiritual Guide, 1833
     Vedanayagam Samuel Azariah, Bishop in South India, Evangelist, 1945
30   Charles, King and Martyr, 1649

February
6   *The Martyrs of Japan, 1597*
27   George Herbert, Priest, Poet, 1633

March
20   Cuthbert, Bishop of Lindisfarne, Missionary, 687

April
10   William Law, Priest, Spiritual Writer, 1761
     William of Ockham, Friar, Philosopher, Teacher, 1347
19   Alphege, Archbishop of Canterbury, Martyr, 1012
21   Anselm, Abbot of Le Bec, Archbishop of Canterbury, Teacher, 1109
24   *Mellitus, Bishop of London, first Bishop at St Paul's, 624*
27   *Christina Rossetti, Poet, 1894*
28   *Peter Chanel, Missionary in the South Pacific, Martyr, 1841*
29   Catherine of Siena, Teacher, 1380
30   *Pandita Mary Ramabai, Translator of the Scriptures, 1922*

May
4   English Saints and Martyrs of the Reformation Era
8   Julian of Norwich, Spiritual Writer, c. 1417

June
5   Boniface (Wynfrith) of Crediton, Bishop, Apostle of Germany, Martyr, 754
19   *Sundar Singh of India, Sadhu (holy man), Evangelist, Teacher, 1929*

July
31   *Ignatius of Loyola, Founder of the Society of Jesus, 1556*

August
7   *John Mason Neale, Priest, Hymn Writer, 1866*
14   *Maximilian Kolbe, Friar, Martyr, 1941*
28   Augustine, Bishop of Hippo, Teacher, 430

September
4   *Birinus, Bishop of Dorchester (Oxon), Apostle of Wessex, 650*
25   Lancelot Andrewes, Bishop of Winchester, Spiritual Writer, 1626
     Sergei of Radonezh, Russian Monastic Reformer, Teacher, 1392

October

9   *Denys, Bishop of Paris, and his Companions, Martyrs, c. 250*
     Robert Grosseteste, Bishop of Lincoln, Philosopher, Scientist, 1253
16   *Nicholas Ridley, Bishop of London, and Hugh Latimer, Bishop of Worcester, Reformation Martyrs, 1555*

November

6   *Leonard, Hermit, 6th century*
     William Temple, Archbishop of Canterbury, Teacher, 1944
13   *Charles Simeon, Priest, Evangelical Divine, 1836*
20   *Edmund, King of the East Angles, Martyr, 870*
     Priscilla Lydia Sellon, a Restorer of the Religious Life in the Church of England, 1876

December

4   *John of Damascus, Monk, Teacher, c. 749*
     Nicholas Ferrar, Deacon, Founder of the Little Gidding Community, 1637

Book of Common Prayer

2011

January
30   Charles, King and Martyr, 1649

April
3   Richard, Bishop of Chichester, 1253
19   Alphege, Archbishop of Canterbury, Martyr, 1012
21   Anselm, Abbot of Le Bec, Archbishop of Canterbury, Teacher, 1109
23   George, Martyr, Patron of England, c. 304

May
3   The Invention of the Cross

June
5   Boniface (Wynfrith) of Crediton, Bishop, Apostle of Germany, Martyr, 754

August
7   The Name of Jesus
28   Augustine, Bishop of Hippo, Teacher, 430

October
9   Denys, Bishop of Paris, Martyr, c. 250

November
6   Leonard, Hermit, 6th century
13   Britius, Bishop of Tours, 444
20   Edmund, King of the East Angles, Martyr, 870

THE COMMON OF THE SAINTS

The Blessed Virgin Mary

Genesis 3. 8–15, 20; Isaiah 7. 10–14; Micah 5. 1–4
Psalms 45. 10–17; 113; 131
Acts 1. 12–14; Romans 8. 18–30; Galatians 4. 4–7
Luke 1. 26–38; Luke 1. 39–47; John 19. 25–27

Martyrs

2 Chronicles 24. 17–21; Isaiah 43. 1–7; Jeremiah 11. 18–20; Wisdom 4. 10–15
Psalms 3; 11; 31. 1–5; 44. 18–24; 126
Romans 8. 35–end; 2 Corinthians 4. 7–15; 2 Timothy 2. 3–7 [8–13]; Hebrews 11. 32–end; 1 Peter
4. 12–end; Revelation 12. 10–12a
Matthew 10. 16–22; Matthew 10. 28–39; Matthew 16. 24–26; John 12. 24–26; John 15. 18–21

Teachers of the Faith and Spiritual Writers

1 Kings 3. [6–10] 11–14; Proverbs 4. 1–9; Wisdom 7. 7–10, 15–16; Ecclesiasticus 39. 1–10
Psalms 19. 7–10; 34. 11–17; 37. 31–35; 119. 89–96; 119. 97–104
1 Corinthians 1. 18–25; 1 Corinthians 2. 1–10; 1 Corinthians 2. 9–end;
Ephesians 3. 8–12; 2 Timothy 4. 1–8; Titus 2. 1–8
Matthew 5. 13–19; Matthew 13. 52–end; Matthew 23. 8–12; Mark 4. 1–9; John 16. 12–15

Bishops and Other Pastors

1 Samuel 16. 1, 6–13; Isaiah 6. 1–8; Jeremiah 1. 4–10; Ezekiel 3. 16–21; Malachi 2. 5–7
Psalms 1; 15; 16. 5–end; 96; 110
Acts 20. 28–35; 1 Corinthians 4. 1–5; 2 Corinthians 4. 1–10 (or 1–2, 5–7); 2 Corinthians 5. 14–20;
1 Peter 5. 1–4
Matthew 11. 25–end; Matthew 24. 42–46; John 10. 11–16; John 15. 9–17; John 21. 15–17

Members of Religious Communities

1 Kings 19. 9–18; Proverbs 10. 27–end; Song of Solomon 8. 6–7; Isaiah 61.10 – 62.5; Hosea 2.
14–15, 19–20
Psalms 34. 1–8; 112. 1–9; 119. 57–64; 123; 131
Acts 4. 32–35; 2 Corinthians 10.17 – 11.2; Philippians 3. 7–14; 1 John 2. 15–17; Revelation 19. 1,
5–9
Matthew 11. 25–end; Matthew 19. 3–12; Matthew 19. 23–end; Luke 9. 57– end; Luke 12. 32–37

Missionaries

Isaiah 52. 7–10; Isaiah 61. 1–3a; Ezekiel 34. 11–16; Jonah 3. 1–5
Psalms 67; 87; 97; 100; 117
Acts 2. 14, 22–36; Acts 13. 46–49; Acts 16. 6–10; Acts 26. 19–23; Romans 15. 17–21;
2 Corinthians 5.11 – 6.2
Matthew 9. 35–end; Matthew 28. 16–end; Mark 16. 15–20; Luke 5. 1–11; Luke 10. 1–9

Any Saint

Genesis 12. 1–4; Proverbs 8. 1–11; Micah 6. 6–8; Ecclesiasticus 2. 7–13 [14–end]
Psalms 32; 33. 1–5; 119. 1–8; 139. 1–4 [5–12]; 145. 8–14
Ephesians 3. 14–19; Ephesians 6. 11–18; Hebrews 13. 7–8, 15–16; James 2. 14–17; 1 John 4. 7–16;
Revelation 21. [1–4] 5–7
Matthew 19. 16–21; Matthew 25. 1–13; Matthew 25. 14–30; John 15. 1–8; John 17. 20–end

SPECIAL OCCASIONS

The Guidance of the Holy Spirit
Proverbs 24. 3–7; Isaiah 30. 15–21; Wisdom 9. 13–17
Psalms 25. 1–9; 104. 26–33; 143. 8–10
Acts 15. 23–29; Romans 8. 22–27; 1 Corinthians 12. 4–13
Luke 14. 27–33; John 14. 23–26; John 16. 13–15

The Commemoration of the Faithful Departed
Lamentations 3. 17–26, 31–33 or Wisdom 3. 1–9
Psalm 23 or Psalm 27. 1–6, 16–end
Romans 5. 5–11 or 1 Peter 1. 3–9
John 5. 19–25 or John 6. 37–40

Rogation Days
Deuteronomy 8. 1–10; 1 Kings 8. 35–40; Job 28. 1–11
Psalms 104. 21–30; 107. 1–9; 121
Philippians 4. 4–7; 2 Thessalonians 3. 6–13; 1 John 5. 12–15
Matthew 6. 1–15; Mark 11. 22–24; Luke 11. 5–13

Harvest Thanksgiving
Year A
Deuteronomy 8. 7–18 or Deuteronomy 28. 1–14
Psalm 65
2 Corinthians 9. 6–end
Luke 12. 16–30 or Luke 17. 11–19

Year B
Joel 2. 21–27
Psalm 126
1 Timothy 2. 1–7 or 1 Timothy 6. 6–10
Matthew 6. 25–33

Year C
Deuteronomy 26. 1–11
Psalm 100
Philippians 4. 4–9 or Revelation 14. 14–18
John 6. 25–35

Mission and Evangelism
Isaiah 49. 1–6; Isaiah 52. 7–10; Micah 4. 1–5
Psalms 2; 46; 67
Acts 17. 12–end; 2 Corinthians 5.14 – 6.2; Ephesians 2. 13–end
Matthew 5. 13–16; Matthew 28. 16–end; John 17. 20– end

The Unity of the Church
Jeremiah 33. 6–9a; Ezekiel 36. 23–28; Zephaniah 3. 16–end
Psalms 100; 122; 133
Ephesians 4. 1–6; Colossians 3. 9–17; 1 John 4. 9–15
Matthew 18. 19–22; John 11. 45–52; John 17. 11b–23

The Peace of the World

Isaiah 9. 1–6; Isaiah 57. 15–19; Micah 4. 1–5

Psalms 40. 14–17; 72. 1–7; 85. 8–13

Philippians 4. 6–9; 1 Timothy 2. 1–6; James 3. 13–18

Matthew 5. 43–end; John 14. 23–29; John 15. 9–17

Social Justice and Responsibility

Isaiah 32. 15–end; Amos 5. 21–24; Amos 8. 4–7; Acts 5. 1–11

Psalms 31. 21–24; 85. 1–7; 146. 5–10

Colossians 3. 12–15; James 2. 1–4

Matthew 5. 1–12; Matthew 25. 31–end; Luke 16. 19–end

Ministry (including Ember Days)

Numbers 11. 16–17, 24–29; Numbers 27. 15–end; 1 Samuel 16. 1–13a

Isaiah 6. 1–8; Isaiah 61. 1–3; Jeremiah 1. 4–10

Psalms 40. 8–13; 84. 8–12; 89. 19–25; 101. 1–5, 7; 122

Acts 20. 28–35; 1 Corinthians 3. 3–11; Ephesians 4. 4–16; Philippians 3. 7–14

Luke 4. 16–21; Luke 12. 35–43; Luke 22. 24–27; John 4. 31–38; John 15. 5–17

In Time of Trouble

Genesis 9. 8–17; Job 1. 13–end; Isaiah 38. 6–11

Psalms 86. 1–7; 107. 4–15; 142. 1–7

Romans 3. 21–26; Romans 8. 18–25; 2 Corinthians 8. 1–5, 9

Mark 4. 35–end; Luke 12. 1–7; John 16. 31–end

For the Sovereign

Joshua 1. 1–9; Proverbs 8. 1–16

Psalms 20; 101; 121

Romans 13. 1–10; Revelation 21.22 – 22.4

Matthew 22. 16–22; Luke 22. 24–30

November 2010

			Sunday Principal Service Weekday Eucharist	Third Service Morning Prayer
28	S	THE FIRST SUNDAY OF ADVENT CW Year A begins		
			Isa. 2. 1–5 Ps. 122 Rom. 13. 11–end	Ps. 44 Mic. 4. 1–7 1 Thess. 5. 1–11
	P		Matt. 24. 36–44	
29	M	Daily Eucharistic Lectionary Year 1 begins		
			Isa. 4. 2–end Ps. 122 Matt. 8. 5–11	Ps. *50*; 54 *alt.* Ps. *1*; 2; 3 Isa. 42. 18–end Rev. ch. 19
		Day of Intercession and Thanksgiving for the Missionary Work of the Church		
			Isa. 49. 1–6; Isa. 52. 7–10; Mic. 4. 1–5 Acts 17. 12–end; 2 Cor. 5.14 – 6.2; Eph. 2. 13–end Ps. 2; 46; 47 Matt. 5. 13–16; Matt. 28.	
	P		16–end; John 17. 20–end	
30	Tu	ANDREW THE APOSTLE		
			Isa. 52. 7–10 Ps. 19. 1–6 Rom. 10. 12–18	*MP:* Ps. 47; 147. 1–12 Ezek. 47. 1–12 *or* Ecclus. 14. 20–end
	R		Matt. 4. 18–22	John 12. 20–32

December 2010

1	W	*Charles de Foucauld, Hermit in the Sahara, 1916*		
			Isa. 25. 6–10a Ps. 23 Matt. 15. 29–37	Ps. 5; *7* *alt.* Ps. 119. 1–32 Isa. 43. 14–end
	P			Rev. 21. 1–8
2	Th		Isa. 26. 1–6 Ps. 118. 18–27a Matt. 7. 21, 24–27	Ps. *42*; 43 *alt.* Ps. 14; *15*; 16 Isa. 44. 1–8
	P			Rev. 21. 9–21
3	F	*Francis Xavier, Missionary, Apostle of the Indies, 1552*		
			Isa. 29. 17–end Ps. 27. 1–4, 16–17 Matt. 9. 27–31	Ps. *25*; 26 *alt.* Ps. 17; *19* Isa. 44. 9–23
	P			Rev. 21.22 – 22.5
4	Sa	*John of Damascus, Monk, Teacher, c. 749; Nicholas Ferrar, Deacon, Founder of the Little Gidding* *Community, 1637*		
			Isa. 30. 19–21, 23–26 Ps. 146. 4–9 Matt. 9.35 – 10.1, 6–8	Ps. *9*; (10) *alt.* Ps. 20; 21; *23* Isa. 44.24 – 45.13
	P			Rev. 22. 6–end
5	S	THE SECOND SUNDAY OF ADVENT		
			Isa. 11. 1–10 Ps. 72. 1–7, 18–19 (*or* 72. 1–7) Rom. 15. 4–13	Ps. 80 Amos ch. 7 Luke 1. 5–20
	P		Matt. 3. 1–12	

Second Service Evening Prayer		Calendar and Holy Communion	Morning Prayer	Evening Prayer
Ps. 9 (or 9. 1–8) Isa. 52. 1–12 Matt. 24. 15–28	P	**THE FIRST SUNDAY OF ADVENT** Advent 1 Collect until Christmas Eve Mic. 4. 1–4, 6–7 Ps. 25. 1–9 Rom. 13. 8–14 Matt. 21. 1–13	Ps. 44 Isa. 2. 1–5 1 Thess. 5. 1–11	Ps. 9 (or 9. 1–8) Isa. 52. 1–12 Matt. 24. 15–28
Ps. 70; **71** alt. Ps. **4**; 7 Isa. 25. 1–9 Matt. 12. 1–21 or First EP of Andrew the Apostle (Ps. 48) Isa. 49. 1–9a 1 Cor. 4. 9–16 **R** ct			Isa. 42. 18–end Rev. ch. 19	Isa. 25. 1–9 Matt. 12. 1–21 or First EP of Andrew the Apostle Ps. 48 Isa. 49. 1–9a 1 Cor. 4. 9–16
	P	To celebrate the Day of Intercession and Thanksgiving for the Missionary Work of the Church, see *Common Worship* provision.		**R** ct
EP: Ps. 87; 96 Zech. 8. 20–end John 1. 35–42	R	**ANDREW THE APOSTLE** Zech. 8. 20–end Ps. 92. 1–5 Rom. 10. 9–end Matt. 4. 18–22	(Ps. 47; 147. 1–12) Ezek. 47. 1–12 or Ecclus. 14. 20–end John 12. 20–32	(Ps. 87; 96) Isa. 52. 7–10 John 1. 35–42
Ps. 76; **77** alt. Ps. **11**; 12; 13 Isa. 28. 1–13 Matt. 12. 38–end	P		Isa. 43. 14–end Rev. 21. 1–8	Isa. 28. 1–13 Matt. 12. 38–end
Ps. **40**; 46 alt. Ps. 18† Isa. 28. 14–end Matt. 13. 1–23	P		Isa. 44. 1–8 Rev. 21. 9–21	Isa. 28. 14–end Matt. 13. 1–23
Ps. 16; **17** alt. Ps. 22 Isa. 29. 1–14 Matt. 13. 24–43	P		Isa. 44. 9–23 Rev. 21.22 – 22.5	Isa. 29. 1–14 Matt. 13. 24–43
Ps. **27**; 28 alt. Ps. **24**; 25 Isa. 29. 15–end Matt. 13. 44–end ct	P		Isa. 44.24 – 45.13 Rev. 22. 6–end	Isa. 29. 15–end Matt. 13. 44–end ct
Ps. 11; [28] 1 Kings 18. 17–39 John 1. 19–28	P	**THE SECOND SUNDAY OF ADVENT** 2 Kings 22. 8–10; 23. 1–3 Ps. 50. 1–6 Rom. 15. 4–13 Luke 21. 25–33	Ps. 80 Amos ch. 7 Luke 1. 5–20	Ps. 11; [28] 1 Kings 18. 17–39 Matt. 3. 1–12

December 2010

			Sunday Principal Service Weekday Eucharist	Third Service Morning Prayer
6	M	**Nicholas, Bishop of Myra, c. 326**		
		Com. Bishop *or*	Isa. ch. 35	Ps. 44
		also Isa. 61. 1–3	Ps. 85. 7–end	*alt.* Ps. 27; **30**
		1 Tim. 6. 6–11	Luke 5. 17–26	Isa. 45. 14–end
	Pw	Mark 10. 13–16		1 Thess. ch. 1
7	Tu	**Ambrose, Bishop of Milan, Teacher, 397**		
		Com. Teacher *or*	Isa. 40. 1–11	Ps. **56**; 57
		also Isa. 41. 9b–13	Ps. 96. 1, 10–end	*alt.* Ps. 32; **36**
		Luke 22. 24–30	Matt. 18. 12–14	Isa. ch. 46
	Pw			1 Thess. 2. 1–12
8	W	**The Conception of the Blessed Virgin Mary**		
		Ember Day*		
		Com. BVM *or*	Isa. 40. 25–end	Ps. **62**; 63
			Ps. 103. 8–13	*alt.* Ps. 34
			Matt. 11. 28–end	Isa. ch. 47
	Pw			1 Thess. 2. 13–end
9	Th		Isa. 41. 13–20	Ps. 53; **54**; 60
			Ps. 145. 1, 8–13	*alt.* Ps. 37†
			Matt. 11. 11–15	Isa. 48. 1–11
	P			1 Thess. ch. 3
10	F	Ember Day*		
			Isa. 48. 17–19	Ps. 85; **86**
			Ps. 1	*alt.* Ps. 31
			Matt. 11. 16–19	Isa. 48. 12–end
	P			1 Thess. 4. 1–12
11	Sa	Ember Day*		
			Ecclus. 48. 1–4, 9–11	Ps. 145
			or 2 Kings 2. 9–12	*alt.* Ps. 41; **42**; 43
			Ps. 80. 1–4, 18–19	Isa. 49. 1–13
			Matt. 17. 10–13	1 Thess. 4. 13–end
	P			
12	S	THE THIRD SUNDAY OF ADVENT		
			Isa. 35. 1–10	Ps. 68. 1–19
			Ps. 146. 4–10	Zeph. 3. 14–end
			or Canticle: Magnificat	Phil. 4. 4–7
			James 5. 7–10	
	P		Matt. 11. 2–11	
13	M	**Lucy, Martyr at Syracuse, 304**		
		Samuel Johnson, Moralist, 1784		
		Com. Martyr *or*	Num. 24. 2–7, 15–17	Ps. 40
		also Wisd. 3. 1–7	Ps. 25. 3–8	*alt.* Ps. 44
		2 Cor. 4. 6–15	Matt. 21. 23–27	Isa. 49. 14–25
	Pr			1 Thess. 5. 1–11
14	Tu	**John of the Cross, Poet, Teacher, 1591**		
		Com. Teacher *or*	Zeph. 3. 1–2, 9–13	Ps. **70**; 74
		esp. 1 Cor. 2. 1–10	Ps. 34. 1–6, 21–22	*alt.* Ps. **48**; 52
		also John 14. 18–23	Matt. 21. 28–32	Isa. ch. 50
	Pw			1 Thess. 5. 12–end
15	W		Isa. 45. 6b–8, 18, 21b–end	Ps. **75**; 96
			Ps. 85. 7–end	*alt.* Ps. 119. 57–80
			Luke 7. 18b–23	Isa. 51. 1–8
	P			2 Thess. ch. 1
16	Th		Isa. 54. 1–10	Ps. **76**; 97
			Ps. 30. 1–5, 11–end	*alt.* Ps. 56; **57**; (63†)
			Luke 7. 24–30	Isa. 51. 9–16
	P			2 Thess. ch. 2

*For Ember Day provision, see p. 13.

Second Service Evening Prayer	Calendar and Holy Communion	Morning Prayer	Evening Prayer
Nicholas, Bishop of Myra, c. 326			
Ps. *144*; 146 *alt.* Ps. 26; *28*; 29 Isa. 30. 1–18 Matt. 14. 1–12	Com. Bishop Pw	Isa. 45. 14–end I Thess. ch. 1	Isa. 30. 1–18 Matt. 14. 1–12
Ps. *11*; 12; 13 *alt.* Ps. 33 Isa. 30. 19–end Matt. 14. 13–end	 P	Isa. ch. 46 I Thess. 2. 1–12	Isa. 30. 19–end Matt. 14. 13–end
The Conception of the Blessed Virgin Mary			
Ps. *10*; 14 *alt.* Ps. 119. 33–56 Isa. ch. 31 Matt. 15. 1–20	 Pw	Isa. ch. 47 I Thess. 2. 13–end	Isa. ch. 31 Matt. 15. 1–20
Ps. 73 *alt.* Ps. 39; *40* Isa. ch. 32 Matt. 15. 21–28	 P	Isa. 48. 1–11 I Thess. ch. 3	Isa. ch. 32 Matt. 15. 21–28
Ps. 82; *90* *alt.* Ps. 35 Isa. 33. 1–22 Matt. 15. 29–end	 P	Isa. 48. 12–end I Thess. 4. 1–12	Isa. 33. 1–22 Matt. 15. 29–end
Ps. 93; *94* *alt.* Ps. 45; *46* Isa. ch. 35 Matt. 16. 1–12 ct	 P	Isa. 49. 1–13 I Thess. 4. 13–end	Isa. ch. 35 Matt. 16. 1–12 ct
Ps. 12; [14] Isa. 5. 8–end Acts 13. 13–41 *Gospel*: John 5. 31–40	**THE THIRD SUNDAY OF ADVENT** Isa. ch. 35 Ps. 80. 1–7 I Cor. 4. 1–5 Matt. 11. 2–10 P	Ps. 68. 1–19 Zeph. 3. 14–end James 5. 7–10	Ps. 12; [14] Isa. 5. 8–end Acts 13. 13–41
Lucy, Martyr at Syracuse, 304			
Ps. 25; *26* *alt.* Ps. *47*; 49 Isa. 38. 1–8, 21–22 Matt. 16. 13–end	Com. Virgin Martyr Pr	Isa. 49. 14–25 I Thess. 5. 1–11	Isa. 38. 1–8, 21–22 Matt. 16. 13–end
Ps. *50*; 54 *alt.* Ps. 50 Isa. 38. 9–20 Matt. 17. 1–13	 P	Isa. ch. 50 I Thess. 5. 12–end	Isa. 38. 9–20 Matt. 17. 1–13
Ps. 25; *82* *alt.* Ps. *59*; 60; (67) Isa. ch. 39 Matt. 17. 14–21	Ember Day Ember CEG P	Isa. 51. 1–8 2 Thess. ch. 1	Isa. ch. 39 Matt. 17. 14–21
Ps. 44 *alt.* Ps. 61; *62*; 64 Zeph. 1.1 – 2.3 Matt. 17. 22–end	O Sapientia P	Isa. 51. 9–16 2 Thess. ch. 2	Zeph. 1.1 – 2.3 Matt. 17. 22–end

December 2010

			Sunday Principal Service Weekday Eucharist	Third Service Morning Prayer
17	F P	O Sapientia *Eglantyne Jebb, Social Reformer, Founder of 'Save the Children', 1928*	Gen. 49. 2, 8–10 Ps. 72. 1–5, 18–19 Matt. 1. 1–17	Ps. 77; **98** *alt.* Ps. **51**; 54 Isa. 51. 17–end 2 Thess. ch. 3
18	Sa P		Jer. 23. 5–8 Ps. 72. 1–2, 12–13, 18–end Matt. 1. 18–24	Ps. 71 *alt.* Ps. 68 Isa. 52. 1–12 Jude
19	S P	THE FOURTH SUNDAY OF ADVENT	Isa. 7. 10–16 Ps. 80. 1–8, 18–20 (*or* 80. 1–8) Rom. 1. 1–7 Matt. 1. 18–end	Ps. 144 Mic. 5. 2–5a Luke 1. 26–38
20	M P		Isa. 7. 10–14 Ps. 24. 1–6 Luke 1. 26–38	Ps. **46**; 95 Isa. 52.13 – 53.end 2 Pet. 1. 1–15
21	Tu* P		Zeph. 3. 14–18 Ps. 33. 1–4, 11–12, 20–end Luke 1. 39–45	Ps. **121**; 122; 123 Isa. ch. 54 2 Pet. 1.16 – 2.3
22	W P		1 Sam. 1. 24–end Ps. 113 Luke 1. 46–56	Ps. **124**; 125; 126; 127 Isa. ch. 55 2 Pet. 2. 4–end
23	Th P		Mal. 3. 1–4; 4. 5–end Ps. 25. 3–9 Luke 1. 57–66	Ps. 128; 129; **130**; 131 Isa. ch. 56. 1–8 2 Pet. ch. 3
24	F P	CHRISTMAS EVE	*Morning Eucharist* 2 Sam. 7. 1–5, 8–11, 16 Ps. 89. 2, 19–27 Acts 13. 16–26 Luke 1. 67–79	Ps. **45**; 113 Isa. 63. 1–6 2 John
25	Sa ꝃ	**CHRISTMAS DAY** *Any of the following sets of readings may be used on the evening of Christmas Eve and on Christmas Day. Set III should be used at some service during the celebration.*	I Isa. 9. 2–7 Ps. 96 Titus 2. 11–14 Luke 2. 1–14 [15–20] II Isa. 62. 6–end Ps. 97 Titus 3. 4–7 Luke 2. [1–7] 8–20 III Isa. 52. 7–10 Ps. 98 Heb. 1. 1–4 [5–12] John 1. 1–14	MP: Ps. **110**; 117 Isa. 62. 1–5 Matt. 1. 18–end

*Thomas the Apostle may be celebrated on 21 December instead of 3 July.

Second Service Evening Prayer		Calendar and Holy Communion	Morning Prayer	Evening Prayer
Ps. 49 *alt.* Ps. 38 Zeph. 3. 1–13 Matt. 18. 1–20	P	Ember Day Ember CEG	Isa. 51. 17–end 2 Thess. ch. 3	Zeph. 3. 1–13 Matt. 18. 1–20
Ps. 42; *43* *alt.* Ps. 65; *66* Zeph. 3. 14–end Matt. 18. 21–end ct	P	Ember Day Ember CEG	Isa. 52. 1–12 Jude	Zeph. 3. 14–end Matt. 18. 21–end ct
Ps. 113; [126] 1 Sam. 1. 1–20 Rev. 22. 6–end *Gospel:* Luke 1. 39–45	P	**THE FOURTH SUNDAY OF ADVENT** Isa. 40. 1–9 Ps. 145. 17–end Phil. 4. 4–7 John 1. 19–28	Ps. 144 Mic. 5. 2–5a Luke 1. 26–38	Ps. 113; [126] 1 Sam. 1. 1–20 Rev. 22. 6–end
Ps. *4*; 9 Mal. 1. 1, 6–end Matt. 19. 1–12	P		Isa. 52.13 – 53.end 2 Pet. 1. 1–15	Mal. 1. 1, 6–end Matt. 19. 1–12 *or First EP of Thomas* (Ps. 27) Isa. ch. 35 Heb. 10.35 – 11.1 R ct
Ps. 80; *84* Mal. 2. 1–16 Matt. 19. 13–15	R	**THOMAS THE APOSTLE** Job 42. 1–6 Ps. 139. 1–11 Eph. 2. 19–end John 20. 24–end	(Ps. 92; 146) 2 Sam. 15. 17–21 *or* Ecclus. ch. 2 John 11. 1–16	(Ps. 139) Hab. 2. 1–4 1 Pet. 1. 3–12
Ps. 24; *48* Mal. 2.17 – 3.12 Matt. 19. 16–end	P		Isa. ch. 55 2 Pet. 2. 4–end	Mal. 2.17 – 3.12 Matt. 19. 16–end
Ps. 89. 1–37 Mal. 3.13 – 4.end Matt. 23. 1–12	P		Isa. ch. 56. 1–8 2 Pet. ch. 3	Mal. 3.13 – 4.end Matt. 23. 1–12
Ps. 85 Zech. ch. 2 Rev. 1. 1–8	P	**CHRISTMAS EVE** Coll. (1) Christmas Eve (2) Advent 1 Mic. 5. 2–5a Ps. 24 Titus 3. 3–7 Luke 2. 1–14	Isa. 63. 1–6 2 John	Zech. ch. 2 Rev. 1. 1–8
EP: Ps. 8 Isa. 65. 17–25 Phil. 2. 5–11 *or* Luke 2. 1–20 *if it has not been used at the principal service of the day*	₩	**CHRISTMAS DAY** Isa. 9. 2–7 Ps. 98 Heb. 1. 1–12 John 1. 1–14	Ps. *110*; 117 Isa. 62. 1–5 Matt. 1. 18–end	Ps. 8 Isa. 65. 17–25 Phil. 2. 5–11 *or* Luke 2. 1–20

December 2010

			Sunday Principal Service **Weekday Eucharist**	**Third Service** **Morning Prayer**

26 S STEPHEN, DEACON, FIRST MARTYR (or transferred to 29th)

    2 Chron. 24. 20–22   MP: Ps. *13*; 31. 1–8; 150
    or Acts 7. 51–end   Jer. 26. 12–15
    Ps. 119. 161–168   Acts ch. 6
    Acts 7. 51–end
    or Gal. 2. 16b–20
    Matt. 10. 17–22

    R

    or, for The First Sunday of Christmas

    Isa. 63. 7–9   Ps. 105. 1–11
    Ps. 148 (or 148. 7–end)   Isa. 35. 1–6
    Heb. 2. 10–end   Gal. 3. 23–end
    W   Matt. 2. 13–end

27 M JOHN, APOSTLE AND EVANGELIST

    Exod. 33. 7–11a   MP: Ps. *21*; 147. 13–end
    Ps. 117   Exod. 33. 12–end
    1 John ch. 1   1 John 2. 1–11
    John 21. 19b–end

    W

28 Tu THE HOLY INNOCENTS

    Jer. 31. 15–17   MP: Ps. *36*; 146
    Ps. 124   Baruch 4. 21–27
    1 Cor. 1. 26–29   or Gen. 37. 13–20
    Matt. 2. 13–18   Matt. 18. 1–10

    R

29 W **Thomas Becket, Archbishop of Canterbury, Martyr, 1170***
    (For Stephen, Deacon, First Martyr, see provision on 26th.)
    Com. Martyr   *or*   1 John 2. 3–11   Ps. *19*; 20
    esp. Matt. 10. 28–33   Ps. 96. 1–4   Isa. 57. 15–end
    Wr   *also* Ecclus. 51. 1–8   Luke 2. 22–35   John 1. 1–18

30 Th

    1 John 2. 12–17   Ps. 111; 112; *113*
    Ps. 96. 7–10   Isa. 59. 1–15a
    W   Luke 2. 36–40   John 1. 19–28

31 F *John Wyclif, Reformer, 1384*

    1 John 2. 18–21   Ps. 102
    Ps. 96. 1, 11–end   Isa. 59. 15b–end
    John 1. 1–18   John 1. 29–34

    W

January 2011

1 Sa THE NAMING AND CIRCUMCISION OF JESUS

    Num. 6. 22–end   MP: Ps. *103*; 150
    Ps. 8   Gen. 17. 1–13
    Gal. 4. 4–7   Rom. 2. 17–end
    Luke 2. 15–21

    W

---

*Thomas Becket may be celebrated on 7 July instead of 29 December.

Second Service Evening Prayer		Calendar and Holy Communion	Morning Prayer	Evening Prayer
EP: Ps. 57; **86** Gen. 4. 1–10 Matt. 23. 34–end		**STEPHEN, DEACON, FIRST MARTYR** (or transferred to 29th) Collect (1) Stephen (2) Christmas 2 Chron. 24. 20–22 Ps. 119. 161–168 Acts 7. 55–end	(Ps. **13**; 31. 1–8; 150) Jer. 26. 12–15 Acts ch. 6	(Ps. 57; **86**) Gen. 4. 1–10 Matt. 10. 17–22
	R	Matt. 23. 34–end		
Ps. 132 Isa. 49. 7–13 Phil. 2. 1–11 Gospel: Luke 2. 41–52		or, for The First Sunday after Christmas Day Isa. 62. 10–12 Ps. 45. 1–7 Gal. 4. 1–7	Ps. 105. 1–11 Isa. 35. 1–6 Gal. 3. 23–end	Ps. 132 Isa. 49. 7–13 Phil. 2. 1–11
	W	Matt. 1. 18–end		
EP: Ps. 97 Isa. 6. 1–8 1 John 5. 1–12		**JOHN, APOSTLE AND EVANGELIST** Collect (1) John (2) Christmas Exod. 33. 18–end Ps. 92. 11–end 1 John ch. 1	(Ps. **21**; 147. 13–end) Exod. 33. 7–11a 1 John 2. 1–11	(Ps. 97) Isa. 6. 1–8 1 John 5. 1–12
	W	John 21. 19b–end		
EP: Ps. 123; **128** Isa. 49. 14–25 Mark 10. 13–16		**THE HOLY INNOCENTS** Collect (1) Innocents (2) Christmas Jer. 31. 10–17 Ps. 123 Rev. 14. 1–5	(Ps. **36**; 146) Baruch 4. 21–27 or Gen. 37. 13–20 Matt. 18. 1–10	(Ps. 124; **128**) Isa. 49. 14–25 Mark 10. 13–16
	R	Matt. 2. 13–18		
Ps. 131; **132** Jonah ch. 1 Col. 1. 1–14			Isa. 57. 15–end John 1. 1–18	Jonah ch. 1 Col. 1. 1–14
	W			
Ps. **65**; 84 Jonah ch. 2 Col. 1. 15–23			Isa. 59. 1–15a John 1. 19–28	Jonah ch. 2 Col. 1. 15–23
	W			
Ps. **90**; 148 Jonah chs 3 & 4 Col. 1.24 – 2.7 or First EP of The Naming of Jesus Ps. 148 Jer. 23. 1–6 Col. 2. 8–15		**Silvester, Bishop of Rome, 335** Com. Bishop	Isa. 59. 15b–end John 1. 29–34	Jonah chs 3 & 4 Col. 1.24 – 2.7 or First EP of The Circumcision of Christ (Ps. 148) Jer. 23. 1–6 Col. 2. 8–15
ct	W			ct
EP: Ps. 115 Deut. 30. [1–10] 11–end Acts 3. 1–16		**THE CIRCUMCISION OF CHRIST** Additional collect Gen. 17. 3b–10 Ps. 98 Rom. 4. 8–13 or Eph. 2. 11–18	(Ps. 103; 150) Gen. 17. 1–13 Rom. 2. 17–end	(Ps. 115) Deut. 30. [1–10] 11–end Acts 3. 1–16
	W	Luke 2. 15–21		

January 2011

			Sunday Principal Service Weekday Eucharist	Third Service Morning Prayer

2   S   **THE SECOND SUNDAY OF CHRISTMAS**
or The Epiphany (*see provision on the 5th and 6th*)

		Sunday Principal Service / Weekday Eucharist	Third Service / Morning Prayer
		Jer. 31. 7–14	Ps. 87
		Ps. 147. 13–end	Jer. 31. 15–17
		or Ecclus. 24. 1–12	2 Cor. 1. 3–12
		Canticle: Wisd. 10. 15–end	
		Eph. 1. 3–14	
W		John 1. [1–9] 10–18	

3   M

	Sunday Principal Service / Weekday Eucharist	Third Service / Morning Prayer
	1 John 2.29 – 3.6	Ps. *127*; 128; 131
	Ps. 98. 2–7	Isa. 60. 13–end
	John 1. 29–34	John 1. 43–end

or, if The Epiphany is celebrated on 2 January:

	Sunday Principal Service / Weekday Eucharist	Third Service / Morning Prayer
	1 John 3.22 – 4.6	Ps. *127*; 128; 131
	Ps. 2. 7–end	*alt.* Ps. 71
	Matt. 4. 12–17, 23–end	Isa. 60. 1–12
W		John 1. 35–42

4   Tu

	Sunday Principal Service / Weekday Eucharist	Third Service / Morning Prayer
	1 John 3. 7–10	Ps. 89. 1–37
	Ps. 98. 1, 8–end	Isa. ch. 61
	John 1. 35–42	John 2. 1–12

or, if The Epiphany is celebrated on 2 January:

	Sunday Principal Service / Weekday Eucharist	Third Service / Morning Prayer
	1 John 4. 7–10	Ps. 89. 1–37
	Ps. 72. 1–8	*alt.* Ps. 73
	Mark 6. 34–44	Isa. 60. 13–end
W		John 1. 43–end

5   W

	Sunday Principal Service / Weekday Eucharist	Third Service / Morning Prayer
	1 John 3. 11–21	Ps. 8; *48*
	Ps. 100	Isa. ch. 62
	John 1. 43–end	John 2. 13–end

or, if The Epiphany is celebrated on 2 January:

	Sunday Principal Service / Weekday Eucharist	Third Service / Morning Prayer
	1 John 4. 11–18	Ps. 8; *48*
	Ps. 72. 1, 10–13	*alt.* Ps. 77
	Mark 6. 45–52	Isa. ch. 61
W		John 2. 1–12

6   Th   **THE EPIPHANY**

	Sunday Principal Service / Weekday Eucharist	Third Service / Morning Prayer
	Isa. 60. 1–6	*MP*: Ps. *132*; 113
	Ps. 72 (or 72. 10–15)	Jer. 31. 7–14
♒	Eph. 3. 1–12	John 1. 29–34
	Matt. 2. 1–12	

or, if The Epiphany is celebrated on 2 January:

	Sunday Principal Service / Weekday Eucharist	Third Service / Morning Prayer
	1 John 4.19 – 5.4	Ps. 18. 1–30
	Ps. 72. 1, 17–end	*alt.* Ps. 78. 1–39†
	Luke 4. 14–22	Isa. ch. 62
W		John 2. 13–end

7   F

	Sunday Principal Service / Weekday Eucharist	Third Service / Morning Prayer
	1 John 3.22 – 4.6	Ps. *99*; 147. 1–12
	Ps. 2. 7–end	*alt.* Ps. 55
	Matt. 4. 12–17, 23–end	Isa. 63. 7–end
		1 John ch. 3

or, if The Epiphany is celebrated on 2 January:

	Sunday Principal Service / Weekday Eucharist	Third Service / Morning Prayer
	1 John 5. 5–13	Ps. *99*; 147. 1–12
	Ps. 147. 13–end	*alt.* Ps. 55
	Luke 5. 12–16	Isa. 63. 7–end
W		1 John ch. 3

Second Service Evening Prayer	Calendar and Holy Communion	Morning Prayer	Evening Prayer
	THE SECOND SUNDAY AFTER CHRISTMAS		
Ps. 135 (or 135. 1–14) Isa. 41.21 – 42.4 Col. 1. 1–14 *Gospel*: Matt. 2. 13–23	Exod. 24. 12–18 Ps. 93 2 Cor. 8. 9 John 1. 14–18 **W**	Ps. 87 Jer. 31. 15–17 2 Cor. 1. 3–12	Ps. 135 (or 135. 1–14) Isa. 41.21 – 42.4 Col. 1. 1–14
Ps. **2**; 110 Ruth ch. 2 Col. 3. 1–11		Isa. 60. 13–end John 1. 43–end	Ruth ch. 2 Col. 3. 1–11
Ps. **2**; 110 *alt.* Ps. **72**; 75 Ruth ch. 1 Col. 2. 8–end	**W**		
Ps. 85; **87** Ruth ch. 3 Col. 3.12 – 4.1		Isa. ch. 61 John 2. 1–12	Ruth ch. 3 Col. 3.12 – 4.1
Ps. 85; **87** *alt.* Ps. 74 Ruth ch. 2 Col. 3. 1–11	**W**		
First EP of The Epiphany Ps. 96; **97** Isa. 49. 1–13 John 4. 7–26 𝖂 ct		Isa. ch. 62 John 2. 13–end	*First EP of The Epiphany* Ps. 96; **97** Isa. 49. 1–13 John 4. 7–26 𝖂 ct
Ps. 45; **46** *alt.* Ps. 119. 81–104 Ruth ch. 3 Col. 3.12 – 4.1	**W**		
EP: Ps. **98**; 100 Baruch 4.36 – 5.end *or* Isa. 60. 1–9 John 2. 1–11	**THE EPIPHANY** Isa. 60. 1–9 Ps. 100 Eph. 3. 1–12 Matt. 2. 1–12	Ps. 132; 113 Jer. 31. 7–14 John 1. 29–34	Ps. 72; 98 Baruch 4.36 – 5.end *or* Isa. 60. 1–9 John 2. 1–11
Ps. 45; **46** *alt.* Ps. 78. 40–end† Ruth 4. 1–17 Col. 4. 2–end	𝖂		
Ps. 118 *alt.* Ps. 69 Baruch 1.15 – 2.10 *or* Jer. 23. 1–8 Matt. 20. 1–16		Isa. 63. 7–end 1 John ch. 3	Baruch 1.15 – 2.10 *or* Jer. 23. 1–8 Matt. 20. 1–16
Ps. 118 *alt.* Ps. 69 Baruch 1.15 – 2.10 *or* Jer. 23. 1–8 Matt. 20. 1–16	**W** or **G**		

January 2011

			Sunday Principal Service Weekday Eucharist	Third Service Morning Prayer
8	Sa		1 John 4. 7–10 Ps. 72. 1–8 Mark 6. 34–44	Ps. *46*; 147. 13–end *alt.* Ps. *76*; 79 Isa. ch. 64 1 John 4. 7–end
		or, if The Epiphany is celebrated on 2 January:	1 John 5. 14–end Ps. 149. 1–5 John 3. 22–30	Ps. *46*; 147. 13–end *alt.* Ps. *76*; 79 Isa. ch. 64 1 John 4. 7–end
	W			
9	S	THE BAPTISM OF CHRIST (THE FIRST SUNDAY OF EPIPHANY)	Isa. 42. 1–9 Ps. 29 Acts 10. 34–43 Matt. 3. 13–end	Ps. 89. 19–29 Exod. 14. 15–22 1 John 5. 6–9
	ꝩ			
10 DEL 1	M	*William Laud, Archbishop of Canterbury, 1645*	Heb. 1. 1–6 Ps. 97. 1–2, 6–10 Mark 1. 14–20	Ps. *2*; 110 *alt.* Ps. *80*; 82 Amos ch. 1
	W			1 Cor. 1. 1–17
11	Tu	*Mary Slessor, Missionary in West Africa, 1915*	Heb. 2. 5–12 Ps. 8 Mark 1. 21–28	Ps. 8; *9* *alt.* Ps. 87; *89. 1–18* Amos ch. 2
	W			1 Cor. 1. 18–end
12	W	**Aelred of Hexham, Abbot of Rievaulx, 1167** *Benedict Biscop, Abbot of Wearmouth, Scholar, 689* Com. Religious *or* *also* Ecclus. 15. 1–6	Heb. 2. 14–end Ps. 105. 1–9 Mark 1. 29–39	Ps. 19; *20* *alt.* Ps. 119. 105–128 Amos ch. 3
	W			1 Cor. ch. 2
13	Th	**Hilary, Bishop of Poitiers, Teacher, 367** *Kentigern (Mungo), Missionary Bishop in Strathclyde and Cumbria, 603; George Fox, Founder of the* *Society of Friends (the Quakers), 1691* Com. Teacher *or* *also* 1 John 2. 18–25	Heb. 3. 7–14 Ps. 95. 1, 8–end Mark 1. 40–end	Ps. *21*; 24 *alt.* Ps. 90; *92* Amos ch. 4
	W	John 8. 25–32		1 Cor. ch. 3
14	F		Heb. 4. 1–5, 11 Ps. 78. 3–8 Mark 2. 1–12	Ps. *67*; 72 *alt.* Ps. *88*; (95) Amos 5. 1–17
	W			1 Cor. ch. 4
15	Sa		Heb. 4. 12–end Ps. 19. 7–end Mark 2. 13–17	Ps. 29; *33* *alt.* Ps. 96; *97*; 100 Amos 5. 18–end
	W			1 Cor. ch. 5

Second Service Evening Prayer	Calendar and Holy Communion	Morning Prayer	Evening Prayer
Ps. 145 *alt*. Ps. 81; *84* Baruch 2. 11–end *or* Jer. 30. 1–17 Matt. 20. 17–28 **ct** *or First EP of The Baptism* *of Christ* Ps. 36 Isa. ch. 61 Titus 2. 11–14; 3. 4–7 ꟼ **ct**	**Lucian, Priest and Martyr, 290** Com. Martyr	Isa. ch. 64 1 John 4. 7–end	Baruch 2. 11–end *or* Jer. 30. 1–17 Matt. 20. 17–28
Ps. 145 *alt*. Ps. 81; *84* Baruch 2. 11–end *or* Jer. 30. 1–17 Matt. 20. 17–28 **ct** *or First EP of The Baptism* *of Christ* ꟼ **ct**	**Wr** *or* **Gr**		**ct**
Ps. 46; 47 Josh. 3. 1–8, 14–end Heb. 1. 1–12 *Gospel:* Luke 3. 15–22	THE FIRST SUNDAY AFTER EPIPHANY To celebrate The Baptism of Christ, see *Common Worship* provision. Zech. 8. 1–8 Ps. 72. 1–8 Rom. 12. 1–5 Luke 2. 41–end	Ps. 89. 19–29 Exod. 14. 15–22 1 John 5. 6–9	Ps. 46; 47 Josh. 3. 1–8, 14–end Heb. 1. 1–12
	W *or* **G**		
Ps. *34*; 36 *alt*. Ps. *85*; 86 Gen. 1. 1–19 Matt. 21. 1–17	**W** *or* **G**	Amos ch. 1 1 Cor. 1. 1–17	Gen. 1. 1–19 Matt. 21. 1–17
Ps. *45*; 46 *alt*. Ps. 89. 19–end Gen. 1.20 – 2.3 Matt. 21. 18–32	**W** *or* **G**	Amos ch. 2 1 Cor. 1. 18–end	Gen. 1.20 – 2.3 Matt. 21. 18–32
Ps. *47*; 48 *alt*. Ps. *91*; 93 Gen. 2. 4–end Matt. 21. 33–end	**W** *or* **G**	Amos ch. 3 1 Cor. ch. 2	Gen. 2. 4–end Matt. 21. 33–end
Ps. *61*; 65 *alt*. Ps. 94 Gen. ch. 3 Matt. 22. 1–14	**Hilary, Bishop of Poitiers, Teacher, 367** Com. Doctor **W** *or* **Gw**	Amos ch. 4 1 Cor. ch. 3	Gen. ch. 3 Matt. 22. 1–14
Ps. 68 *alt*. Ps. 102 Gen. 4. 1–16, 25–26 Matt. 22. 15–33	**W** *or* **G**	Amos 5. 1–17 1 Cor. ch. 4	Gen. 4. 1–16, 25–26 Matt. 22. 15–33
Ps. 84; *85* *alt*. Ps. 104 Gen. 6. 1–10 Matt. 22. 34–end **ct**	**W** *or* **G**	Amos 5. 18–end 1 Cor. ch. 5	Gen. 6. 1–10 Matt. 22. 34–end **ct**

January 2011

		Sunday Principal Service Weekday Eucharist	Third Service Morning Prayer

16   S   THE SECOND SUNDAY OF EPIPHANY

Isa. 49. 1–7
Ps. 40. 1–12
1 Cor. 1. 1–9
John 1. 29–42

Ps. 145. 1–12
Jer. 1. 4–10
Mark 1. 14–20

W

---

17   M
DEL 2

Antony of Egypt, Hermit, Abbot, 356
Charles Gore, Bishop, Founder of the Community of the Resurrection, 1932
Com. Religious   or   Heb. 5. 1–10
esp. Phil. 3. 7–14   Ps. 110. 1–4
also Matt. 19. 16–26   Mark 2. 18–22

Ps. 145; *146*
alt. Ps. *98*; 99; 101
Amos ch. 6
1 Cor. 6. 1–11

W

---

18   Tu

The Week of Prayer for Christian Unity until 25th

Heb. 6. 10–end
Ps. 111
Mark 2. 23–end

Ps. *132*; 147. 1–12
alt. Ps. 106† (or 103)
Amos ch. 7
1 Cor. 6. 12–end

W

---

19   W

Wulfstan, Bishop of Worcester, 1095
Com. Bishop   or   Heb. 7. 1–3, 15–17
esp. Matt. 24. 42–46   Ps. 110. 1–4
     Mark 3. 1–6

Ps. *81*; 147. 13–end
alt. Ps. 110; *111*; 112
Amos ch. 8
1 Cor. 7. 1–24

W

---

20   Th

Richard Rolle of Hampole, Spiritual Writer, 1349
Heb. 7.25 – 8.6
Ps. 40. 7–10, 17–end
Mark 3. 7–12

Ps. *76*; 148
alt. Ps. 113; *115*
Amos ch. 9
1 Cor. 7. 25–end

W

---

21   F

Agnes, Child Martyr at Rome, 304
Com. Martyr   or   Heb. 8. 6–end
also Rev. 7. 13–end   Ps. 85. 7–end
     Mark 3. 13–19

Ps. *27*; 149
alt. Ps. 139
Hos. 1.1 – 2.1
1 Cor. ch. 8

Wr

---

22   Sa

Vincent of Saragossa, Deacon, first Martyr of Spain, 304
Heb. 9. 2–3, 11–14
Ps. 47. 1–8
Mark 3. 20–21

Ps. *122*; 128; 150
alt. Ps. 120; *121*; 122
Hos. 2. 2–17
1 Cor. 9. 1–14

W

---

23   S   THE THIRD SUNDAY OF EPIPHANY

Isa. 9. 1–4
Ps. 27. 1, 4–12 (or 27. 1–11)
1 Cor. 1. 10–18
Matt. 4. 12–23

Ps. 113
Amos 3. 1–8
1 John 1. 1–4

W

---

24   M
DEL 3

Francis de Sales, Bishop of Geneva, Teacher, 1622
Com. Teacher   or   Heb. 9. 15, 24–end
also Prov. 3. 13–18   Ps. 98. 1–7
John 3. 17–21   Mark 3. 22–30

Ps. 40; *108*
alt. Ps. 123; 124; 125; *126*
Hos. 2.18 – 3.end
1 Cor. 9. 15–end

W

---

25   Tu   THE CONVERSION OF PAUL

Jer. 1. 4–10
or Acts 9. 1–22
Ps. 67
Acts 9. 1–22
or Gal. 1. 11–16a
Matt. 19. 27–end

MP: Ps. 66; 147. 13–end
Ezek. 3. 22–end
Phil. 3. 1–14

W

Second Service Evening Prayer	Calendar and Holy Communion	Morning Prayer	Evening Prayer
	THE SECOND SUNDAY AFTER EPIPHANY		
Ps. 96	2 Kings 4. 1–17	Ps. 145. 1–12	Ps. 96
Ezek. 2.1 – 3.4	Ps. 107. 13–22	Jer. 1. 4–10	Ezek. 2.1 – 3.4
Gal. 1. 11–end	Rom. 12. 6–16a	Mark 1. 14–20	Gal. 1. 11–end
Gospel: John 1. 43–end	John 2. 1–11		
	W *or* **G**		
Ps. 71		Amos ch. 6	Gen. 6.11 – 7.10
alt. Ps. 105† (*or* 103)		1 Cor. 6. 1–11	Matt. 24. 1–14
Gen. 6.11 – 7.10			
Matt. 24. 1–14			
	W *or* **G**		
	Prisca, Martyr at Rome, c. 265		
	For the Week of Prayer for Christian Unity, see *Common Worship* provision.		
Ps. 89. 1–37	Com. Virgin Martyr	Amos ch. 7	Gen. 7. 11–end
alt. Ps. 107†		1 Cor. 6. 12–end	Matt. 24. 15–28
Gen. 7. 11–end			
Matt. 24. 15–28			
	Wr *or* **Gr**		
Ps. *97*; 98		Amos ch. 8	Gen. 8. 1–14
alt. Ps. 119. 129–152		1 Cor. 7. 1–24	Matt. 24. 29–end
Gen. 8. 1–14			
Matt. 24. 29–end	**W** *or* **G**		
	Fabian, Bishop of Rome, Martyr, 250		
Ps. 99; 100; *111*	Com. Martyr	Amos ch. 9	Gen. 8.15 – 9.7
alt. Ps. 114; *116*; 117		1 Cor. 7. 25–end	Matt. 25. 1–13
Gen. 8.15 – 9.7			
Matt. 25. 1–13	**Wr** *or* **Gr**		
	Agnes, Child Martyr at Rome, 304		
Ps. 73	Com. Virgin Martyr	Hos. 1.1 – 2.1	Gen. 9. 8–19
alt. Ps. *130*; 131; 137		1 Cor. ch. 8	Matt. 25. 14–30
Gen. 9. 8–19			
Matt. 25. 14–30	**Wr** *or* **Gr**		
	Vincent of Saragossa, Deacon, first Martyr of Spain, 304		
Ps. *61*; 66	Com. Martyr	Hos. 2. 2–17	Gen. 11. 1–9
alt. Ps. 118		1 Cor. 9. 1–14	Matt. 25. 31–end
Gen. 11. 1–9			
Matt. 25. 31–end			
ct	**Wr** *or* **Gr**		ct
	THE THIRD SUNDAY AFTER EPIPHANY		
Ps. 33 (*or* 33. 1–12)	2 Kings 6. 14b–23	Ps. 113	Ps. 33 (*or* 33. 1–12)
Eccles. 3. 1–11	Ps. 102. 15–22	Amos 3. 1–8	Eccles. 3. 1–11
1 Pet. 1. 3–12	Rom. 12. 16b–end	1 John 1. 1–4	1 Pet. 1. 3–12
Gospel: Luke 4. 14–21	Matt. 8. 1–13		
	W *or* **G**		
Ps. *138*; 144		Hos. 2.18 – 3.end	Gen. 11.27 – 12.9
alt. Ps. *127*; 128; 129		1 Cor. 9. 15–end	Matt. 26. 1–16
Gen. 11.27 – 12.9			*or First EP of The*
Matt. 26. 1–16			*Conversion of Paul*
or First EP of The			(Ps. 149)
Conversion of Paul			Isa. 49. 1–13
Ps. 149			Acts 22. 3–16
Isa. 49. 1–13			
Acts 22. 3–16			
ct	**W** *or* **G**		**W** ct
	THE CONVERSION OF PAUL		
EP: Ps. 119. 41–56	Josh. 5. 13–end	(Ps. 66; 147. 13–end)	(Ps. 119. 41–56)
Ecclus. 39. 1–10	Ps. 67	Ezek. 3. 22–end	Ecclus. 39. 1–10
or Isa. 56. 1–8	Acts 9. 1–22	Phil. 3. 1–14	*or* Isa. 56. 1–8
Col. 1.24 – 2.7	Matt. 19. 27–end		Col. 1.24 – 2.7
	W		

January 2011

		Sunday Principal Service Weekday Eucharist	Third Service Morning Prayer

26 W **Timothy and Titus, Companions of Paul**
Isa. 61. 1–3a   *or*   Heb. 10. 11–18   Ps. 45; *46*
Ps. 100   Ps. 110. 1–4   *alt.* Ps. 119. 153–end
2 Tim. 2. 1–8   Mark 4. 1–20   Hos. 5. 1–7
or Titus 1. 1–5   1 Cor. 10.14 – 11.1
W Luke 10. 1–9

27 Th
Heb. 10. 19–25   Ps. *47*; 48
Ps. 24. 1–6   *alt.* Ps. *143*; 146
Mark 4. 21–25   Hos. 5.8 – 6.6
W   1 Cor. 11. 2–16

28 F **Thomas Aquinas, Priest, Philosopher, Teacher, 1274**
Com. Teacher   *or*   Heb. 10. 32–end   Ps. 61; *65*
esp. Wisd. 7. 7–10, 15–16   Ps. 37. 3–6, 40–end   *alt.* Ps. 142; *144*
1 Cor. 2. 9–end   Mark 4. 26–34   Hos. 6.7 – 7.2
W John 16. 12–15   1 Cor. 11. 17–end

29 Sa
Heb. 11. 1–2, 8–19   Ps. 68
Canticle: Luke 1. 69–73 *alt.* Ps. 147
Mark 4. 35–end   Hos. ch. 8
W   1 Cor. 12. 1–11

30 S THE FOURTH SUNDAY OF EPIPHANY
or The Presentation of Christ in the Temple (Candlemas)*
1 Kings 17. 8–16   Ps. 71. 1–6, 15–17
Ps. 36. 5–10   Hag. 2. 1–9
1 Cor. 1. 18–31   1 Cor. 3. 10–17
John 2. 1–11
W

31 M *John Bosco, Priest, Founder of the Salesian Teaching Order, 1888*
DEL 4 (Ordinary Time starts today if The Presentation is observed on 30 January)
Heb. 11. 32–end   Ps. *57*; 96
Ps. 31. 19–end   *alt.* Ps. *1*; 2; 3
Mark 5. 1–20   Hos. ch. 9
W   1 Cor. 12. 12–end

February 2011

1 Tu *Brigid, Abbess of Kildare, c. 525*
Heb. 12. 1–4   Ps. *93*; 97
Ps. 22. 25b–end   *alt.* Ps. *5*; 6; (8)
Mark 5. 21–43   Hos. ch. 10
W   1 Cor. ch. 13

2 W **THE PRESENTATION OF CHRIST IN THE TEMPLE (CANDLEMAS)**
Mal. 3. 1–5   *MP:* Ps. *48*; 146
Ps. 24 (or 24. 7–end)   Exod. 13. 1–16
Heb. 2. 14–end   Rom. 12. 1–5
Luke 2. 22–40

or, if The Presentation is observed on 30 January:
Heb. 12. 4–7, 11–15   Ps. 119. 1–32
Ps. 103. 1–2, 13–18   Hos. 11. 1–11
G Mark 6. 1–6   1 Cor. 14. 1–19

3 Th **Anskar, Archbishop of Hamburg, Missionary in Denmark and Sweden, 865**
Ordinary Time starts today (or on 31 January if The Presentation is observed on 30 January)
Com. Missionary   *or*   Heb. 12. 18–19, 21–24   Ps. 14; *15*; 16
esp. Isa. 52. 7–10   Ps. 48. 1–3, 8–10   Hos. 11.12 – 12.end
Gw *also* Rom. 10. 11–15   Mark 6. 7–13   1 Cor. 14. 20–end

*See provision for First EP on 1 February and throughout the day for The Presentation on 2 February.

Second Service Evening Prayer	Calendar and Holy Communion	Morning Prayer	Evening Prayer
Ps. 21; *29* *alt.* Ps. 136 Gen. ch. 14 Matt. 26. 36–46	W *or* G	Hos. 5. 1–7 I Cor. 10.14 – 11.1	Gen. ch. 14 Matt. 26. 36–46
Ps. *24*; 33 *alt.* Ps. *138*; 140; 141 Gen. ch. 15 Matt. 26. 47–56	W *or* G	Hos. 5.8 – 6.6 I Cor. 11. 2–16	Gen. ch. 15 Matt. 26. 47–56
Ps. *67*; 77 *alt.* Ps. 145 Gen. ch. 16 Matt. 26. 57–end	W *or* G	Hos. 6.7 – 7.2 I Cor. 11. 17–end	Gen. ch. 16 Matt. 26. 57–end
Ps. *72*; 76 *alt.* Ps. *148*; 149; 150 Gen. 17. 1–22 Matt. 27. 1–10 ct	W *or* G	Hos. ch. 8 I Cor. 12. 1–11	Gen. 17. 1–22 Matt. 27. 1–10 ct
	THE FOURTH SUNDAY AFTER EPIPHANY		
Ps. 34 (*or* 34. 1–10) Gen. 28. 10–22 Philemon 1–16 *Gospel:* Mark 1. 21–28	I Sam. 10. 17–24 Ps. 97 Rom. 13. 1–7 Matt. 8. 23–34 W *or* G	Ps. 71. 1–6, 15–17 Hag. 2. 1–9 I Cor. 3. 10–17	Ps. 34 (*or* 34. 1–10) Gen. 28. 10–22 Philemon 1–16
Ps. 2; *20* *alt.* Ps. *4*; 7 Gen. 18. 1–15 Matt. 27. 11–26	W *or* G	Hos. ch. 9 I Cor. 12. 12–end	Gen. 18. 1–15 Matt. 27. 11–26
First EP of The Presentation Ps. 118 I Sam. 1. 19b–end Heb. 4. 11–end 𝖂 ct *or, if The Presentation* *is kept on 30 January:* Ps. *9*; 10† Gen. 18. 16–end Matt. 27. 27–44	W *or* G	Hos. ch. 10 I Cor. ch. 13	*First EP of The Presentation* Ps. 118 I Sam. 1. 19b–end Heb. 4. 11–end 𝖂 ct
	THE PRESENTATION OF CHRIST IN THE TEMPLE		
EP: Ps. 122; *132* Hag. 2. 1–9 John 2. 18–22	Mal. 3. 1–5 Ps. 48; 146 Gal. 4. 1–7 Luke 2. 22–40	Ps. 48; 146 Exod. 13. 1–16 Rom. 12. 1–5	Ps. 122; 132 Hag. 2. 1–9 John 2. 18–22
Ps. *11*; 12; 13 Gen. 19. 1–3, 12–29 Matt. 27. 45–56	𝖂		
	Blasius, Bishop of Sebastopol, Martyr, c. 316 Com. Martyr		
Ps. 18† Gen. 21. 1–21 Matt. 27. 57–end	Gr	Hos. 11.12 – 12.end I Cor. 14. 20–end	Gen. 21. 1–21 Matt. 27. 57–end

February 2011

			Sunday Principal Service Weekday Eucharist	Third Service Morning Prayer
4	F	*Gilbert of Sempringham, Founder of the Gilbertine Order, 1189*	Heb. 13. 1–8 Ps. 27. 1–6, 9–12	Ps. 17; **19** Hos. 13. 1–14
	G		Mark 6. 14–29	1 Cor. 16. 1–9
5	Sa		Heb. 13. 15–17, 20–21 Ps. 23	Ps. 20; 21; **23** Hos. ch. 14
	G		Mark 6. 30–34	1 Cor. 16. 10–end
6	S	**THE FIFTH SUNDAY BEFORE LENT (Proper 1)** *The Accession of Queen Elizabeth II, 1952*	Isa. 58. 1–9a [9b–12] Ps. 112. 1–9 [–end] 1 Cor. 2. 1–12 [13–end]	Ps. 5; 6 Jer. 26. 1–16 Acts 3. 1–10
	G		Matt. 5. 13–20	
7 DEL 5	M		Gen. 1. 1–19 Ps. 104. 1–2, 6–13, 26	Ps. 27; **30** 1 Chron. 10.1 – 11.9
	G		Mark 6. 53–end	John 13. 1–11
8	Tu		Gen. 1.20 – 2.4a Ps. 8	Ps. 32; **36** 1 Chron. ch. 13
	G		Mark 7. 1–13	John 13. 12–20
9	W		Gen. 2. 4b–9, 15–17 Ps. 104. 11–12, 29–32	Ps. 34 1 Chron. 15.1 – 16.3
	G		Mark 7. 14–23	John 13. 21–30
10	Th	*Scholastica, sister of Benedict, Abbess of Plombariola, c. 543*	Gen. 2. 18–end Ps. 128	Ps. 37† 1 Chron. ch. 17
	G		Mark 7. 24–30	John 13. 31–end
11	F		Gen. 3. 1–8 Ps. 32. 1–8	Ps. 31 1 Chron. 21.1 – 22.1
	G		Mark 7. 31–end	John 14. 1–14
12	Sa		Gen. 3. 9–end Ps. 90. 1–12	Ps. 41; **42**; 43 1 Chron. 22. 2–end
	G		Mark 8. 1–10	John 14. 15–end
13	S	**THE FOURTH SUNDAY BEFORE LENT (Proper 2)**	Deut. 30. 15–end or Ecclus. 15. 15–end Ps. 119. 1–8 1 Cor. 3. 1–9	Ps. 10 Jer. 30. 1–3, 10–22 Acts ch. 6
	G		Matt. 5. 21–37	
14 DEL 6	M	**Cyril and Methodius, Missionaries to the Slavs, 869 and 885** *Valentine, Martyr at Rome, c. 269* Com. Missionaries or *esp.* Isa. 52. 7–10 *also* Rom. 10. 11–15	Gen. 4. 1–15, 25 Ps. 50. 1, 8, 16–end Mark 8. 11–13	Ps. 44 1 Chron. 28. 1–10 John 15. 1–11
	Gw			
15	Tu	*Sigfrid, Bishop, Apostle of Sweden, 1045; Thomas Bray, Priest, Founder of the SPCK and SPG, 1730*	Gen. 6. 5–8; 7. 1–5, 10 Ps. 29	Ps. **48**; 52 1 Chron. 28. 11–end
	G		Mark 8. 14–21	John 15. 12–17
16	W		Gen. 8. 6–13, 20–end Ps. 116. 10–end	Ps. 119. 57–80 1 Chron. 29. 1–9
	G		Mark 8. 22–26	John 15. 18–end
17	Th	**Janani Luwum, Archbishop of Uganda, Martyr, 1977** Com. Martyr or *also* Ecclus. 4. 20–28	Gen. 9. 1–13 Ps. 102. 16–23	Ps. 56; **57**; (63†) 1 Chron. 29. 10–20
	Gr	John 12. 24–32	Mark 8. 27–33	John 16. 1–15

Second Service Evening Prayer		Calendar and Holy Communion	Morning Prayer	Evening Prayer
Ps. 22 Gen. 22. 1–19 Matt. 28. 1–15	G		Hos. 13. 1–14 I Cor. 16. 1–9	Gen. 22. 1–19 Matt. 28. 1–15
Ps. 24; 25 Gen. ch. 23 Matt. 28. 16–end ct	Gr	**Agatha, Martyr in Sicily, 251** Com. Virgin Martyr	Hos. ch. 14 I Cor. 16. 10–end	Gen. ch. 23 Matt. 28. 16–end ct
Ps. [1; 3]; 4 Amos 2. 4–end Eph. 4. 17–end Gospel: Mark 1. 29–39	G	THE FIFTH SUNDAY AFTER EPIPHANY **The Accession of Queen Elizabeth II, 1952** Hosea 6. 4–6 Ps. 118. 14–21 Col. 3. 12–17 Matt. 13. 24b–30	Ps. 5; 6 Jer. 26. 1–16 Acts 3. 1–10	Ps. [1; 3]; 4 Amos 2. 4–end Eph. 4. 17–end
Ps. 26; 28; 29 Exod. 22. 21–27; 23. 1–17 Phil. 1. 1–11	G		I Chron. 10.1 – 11.9 John 13. 1–11	Exod. 22. 21–27; 23. 1–17 Phil. 1. 1–11
Ps. 33 Exod. 29.38 – 30.16 Phil. 1. 12–end	G		I Chron. ch. 13 John 13. 12–20	Exod. 29.38 – 30.16 Phil. 1. 12–end
Ps. 119. 33–56 Lev. ch. 8 Phil. 2. 1–13	G		I Chron. 15.1 – 16.3 John 13. 21–30	Lev. ch. 8 Phil. 2. 1–13
Ps. 39; 40 Lev. ch. 9 Phil. 2. 14–end	G		I Chron. ch. 17 John 13. 31–end	Lev. ch. 9 Phil. 2. 14–end
Ps. 35 Lev. 16. 2–24 Phil. 3.1 – 4.1	G		I Chron. 21.1 – 22.1 John 14. 1–14	Lev. 16. 2–24 Phil. 3.1 – 4.1
Ps. 45; 46 Lev. ch. 17 Phil. 4. 2–end ct	G		I Chron. 22. 2–end John 14. 15–end	Lev. ch. 17 Phil. 4. 2–end ct
Ps. [7]; 13 Amos 3. 1–8 Eph. 5. 1–17 Gospel: Mark 1. 40–end	G	THE SIXTH SUNDAY AFTER EPIPHANY Isa. 4. 2–end Ps. 96 I John 3. 1–8 Matt. 24. 23–31	Ps. 10 Jer. 30. 1–3, 10–22 Acts ch. 6	Ps. [7]; 13 Amos 3. 1–8 Eph. 5. 1–17
Ps. 47; 49 Lev. 19. 1–18, 30–end I Tim. 1. 1–17	Gr	**Valentine, Martyr at Rome, c. 269** Com. Martyr	I Chron. 28. 1–10 John 15. 1–11	Lev. 19. 1–18, 30–end I Tim. 1. 1–17
Ps. 50 Lev. 23. 1–22 I Tim. 1.18 – 2.end	G		I Chron. 28. 11–end John 15. 12–17	Lev. 23. 1–22 I Tim. 1.18 – 2.end
Ps. 59; 60; (67) Lev. 23. 23–end I Tim. ch. 3	G		I Chron. 29. 1–9 John 15. 18–end	Lev. 23. 23–end I Tim. ch. 3
Ps. 61; 62; 64 Lev. 24. 1–9 I Tim. ch. 4	G		I Chron. 29. 10–20 John 16. 1–15	Lev. 24. 1–9 I Tim. ch. 4

February 2011

		Sunday Principal Service / Weekday Eucharist	Third Service / Morning Prayer
18	F	Gen. 11. 1–9 Ps. 33. 10–15	Ps. *51*; 54 1 Chron. 29. 21–end
	G	Mark 8.34 – 9.1	John 16. 16–22
19	Sa	Heb. 11. 1–7 Ps. 145. 1–10	Ps. 68 2 Chron. 1. 1–13
	G	Mark 9. 2–13	John 16. 23–end
20	S	THE THIRD SUNDAY BEFORE LENT (Proper 3)	
		Lev. 19. 1–2, 9–18 Ps. 119. 33–40 1 Cor. 3. 10–11, 16–end	Ps. 21; 23 Jer. 33. 1–11 Acts 8. 4–25
	G	Matt. 5. 38–end	
21 DEL 7	M	Ecclus. 1. 1–10 or James 1. 1–11 Ps. 93 or Ps. 119. 65–72	Ps. 71 2 Chron. 2. 1–16 John 17. 1–5
	G	Mark 9. 14–29	
22	Tu	Ecclus. 2. 1–11 or James 1. 12–18 Ps. 37. 3–6, 27–28 or Ps. 94. 12–18	Ps. 73 2 Chron. ch. 3 John 17. 6–19
	G	Mark 9. 30–37	
23	W	**Polycarp, Bishop of Smyrna, Martyr, c. 155** Com. Martyr or *also* Rev. 2. 8–11	Ecclus. 4. 11–19 or James 1. 19–end Ps. 119. 161–168 or Ps. 15 Mark 9. 38–40	Ps. 77 2 Chron. ch. 5 John 17. 20–end
	Gr		
24	Th*	Ecclus. 5. 1–8 or James 2. 1–9 Ps. 1 or Ps. 34. 1–7	Ps. 78. 1–39† 2 Chron. 6. 1–21 John 18. 1–11
	G	Mark 9. 41–end	
25	F	Ecclus. 6. 5–17 or James 2. 14–24, 26 Ps. 119. 19–24 or Ps. 112	Ps. 55 2 Chron. 6. 22–end John 18. 12–27
	G	Mark 10. 1–12	
26	Sa	Ecclus. 17. 1–15 or James 3. 1–10 Ps. 103. 13–18 or Ps. 12. 1–7	Ps. *76*; 79 2 Chron. ch. 7 John 18. 28–end
	G	Mark 10. 13–16	
27	S	THE SECOND SUNDAY BEFORE LENT	
		Gen. 1.1 – 2.3 Ps. 136 or Ps. 136. 1–9, 23–end Rom. 8. 18–25	Ps. 100; 150 Job 38. 1–21 Col. 1. 15–20
	G	Matt. 6. 25–end	
28 DEL 8	M	Ecclus. 17. 24–29 or James 3. 13–end Ps. 32. 1–8 or Ps. 19. 7–end	Ps. *80*; 82 2 Chron. 9. 1–12 John 19. 1–16
	G	Mark 10. 17–27	

*Matthias may be celebrated on 24 February instead of 14 May.

Second Service Evening Prayer		Calendar and Holy Communion	Morning Prayer	Evening Prayer
Ps. 38 Lev. 25. 1–24 1 Tim. 5. 1–16	G		1 Chron. 29. 21–end John 16. 16–22	Lev. 25. 1–24 1 Tim. 5. 1–16
Ps. 65; **66** Num. 6. 1–5, 21–end 1 Tim. 5. 17–end ct	G		2 Chron. 1. 1–13 John 16. 23–end	Num. 6. 1–5, 21–end 1 Tim. 5. 17–end ct
Ps. 18. 1–20 (or 18. 21–30) Amos 9. 5–end Eph. 6. 1–20 *Gospel:* Mark 2. 1–12	G	**SEPTUAGESIMA** Gen. 1. 1–5 Ps. 9. 10–20 1 Cor. 9. 24–end Matt. 20. 1–16	Ps. 21; 23 Jer. 33. 1–11 Acts 8. 4–25	Ps. 18. 1–20 (or 18. 21–30) Amos 9. 5–end Eph. 6. 1–20
Ps. **72**; 75 Gen. 24. 1–28 1 Tim. 6. 1–10	G		2 Chron. 2. 1–16 John 17. 1–5	Gen. 24. 1–28 1 Tim. 6. 1–10
Ps. 74 Gen. 24. 29–end 1 Tim. 6. 11–end	G		2 Chron. ch. 3 John 17. 6–19	Gen. 24. 29–end 1 Tim. 6. 11–end
Ps. 119. 81–104 Gen. 25. 7–11, 19–end 2 Tim. 1. 1–14	G		2 Chron. ch. 5 John 17. 20–end	Gen. 25. 7–11, 19–end 2 Tim. 1. 1–14 *or First EP of Matthias* (Ps. 147) Isa. 22. 15–22 Phil. 3.13b – 4.1 **R** ct
Ps. 78. 40–end† Gen. 26.34 – 27.40 2 Tim. 1.15 – 2.13	R	**MATTHIAS THE APOSTLE** 1 Sam. 2. 27–35 Ps. 16. 1–7 Acts 1. 15–end Matt. 1. 25–end	(Ps. 15) Jonah 1. 1–9 Acts 2. 37–end	(Ps. 80) 1 Sam. 16. 1–13a Matt. 7. 15–27
Ps. 69 Gen. 27.41 – 28.end 2 Tim. 2. 14–end	G		2 Chron. 6. 22–end John 18. 12–27	Gen. 27.41 – 28.end 2 Tim. 2. 14–end
Ps. 81; **84** Gen. 29. 1–30 2 Tim. ch. 3 ct	G		2 Chron. ch. 7 John 18. 28–end	Gen. 29. 1–30 2 Tim. ch. 3 ct
Ps. 148 Prov. 8. 1, 22–31 Rev. ch. 4 *Gospel:* Luke 12. 16–31	G	**SEXAGESIMA** Gen. 3. 9–19 Ps. 83. 1–2, 13–end 2 Cor. 11. 19–31 Luke 8. 4–15	Ps. 100; 150 Job 38. 1–21 Col. 1. 15–20	Ps. 148 Prov. 8. 1, 22–31 Rev. ch. 4
Ps. **85**; 86 Gen. 29.31 – 30.24 2 Tim. 4. 1–8	G		2 Chron. 9. 1–12 John 19. 1–16	Gen. 29.31 – 30.24 2 Tim. 4. 1–8

March 2011

			Sunday Principal Service / Weekday Eucharist	Third Service / Morning Prayer

1 Tu — **David, Bishop of Menevia, Patron of Wales, c. 601**
Com. Bishop *or* Ecclus. 35. 1–12
also 2 Sam. 23. 1–4 *or* James 4. 1–10
Ps. 89. 19–22, 24 Ps. 50. 1–6
or Ps. 55. 7–9, 24
Gw Mark 10. 28–31

Third Service / Morning Prayer:
Ps. 87; **89**. *1–18*
2 Chron. 10.1 – 11.4
John 19. 17–30

---

2 W — **Chad, Bishop of Lichfield, Missionary, 672***
Com. Missionary *or* Ecclus. 36. 1–2, 4–5, 10–17
also 1 Tim. 6. 11b–16 *or* James 4. 13–end
Ps. 79. 8–9, 12, 14
or Ps. 49. 1–2, 5–10
Gw Mark 10. 32–45

Ps. 119. 105–128
2 Chron. ch. 12
John 19. 31–end

---

3 Th
Ecclus. 42. 15–end
or James 5. 1–6
Ps. 33. 1–9
or Ps. 49. 12–20
G Mark 10. 46–end

Ps. 90; **92**
2 Chron. 13.1 – 14.1
John 20. 1–10

---

4 F
Ecclus. 44. 1, 9–13
or James 5. 9–12
Ps. 149. 1–5
or Ps. 103. 1–4, 8–13
G Mark 11. 11–26

Ps. **88**; (95)
2 Chron. 14. 2–end
John 20. 11–18

---

5 Sa
Ecclus. 51. 12–20
or James 5. 13–end
Ps. 19. 7–end
or Ps. 141. 1–4
G Mark 11. 27–end

Ps. 96; **97**; 100
2 Chron. 15. 1–15
John 20. 19–end

---

6 S — THE SUNDAY NEXT BEFORE LENT
Exod. 24. 12–end
Ps. 2
or Ps. 99
2 Pet. 1. 16–end
G Matt. 17. 1–9

Ps. 72
Exod. 34. 29–end
2 Cor. 4. 3–6

---

7 M — **Perpetua, Felicity and their Companions, Martyrs at Carthage, 203**
DEL 9
Com. Martyr *or* Tob. 1. 1–2; 2. 1–8
esp. Rev. 12. 10–12a *or* 1 Pet. 1. 3–9
also Wisd. 3. 1–7 Ps. 15
or Ps. 111
Gr Mark 12. 1–12

Ps. 98; **99**; 101
Jer. ch. 1
John 3. 1–21

---

8 Tu — **Edward King, Bishop of Lincoln, 1910**
Felix, Bishop, Apostle to the East Angles, 647; Geoffrey Studdert Kennedy, Priest, Poet, 1929
Com. Bishop *or* Tob. 2. 9–end
also Heb. 13. 1–8 *or* 1 Pet. 1. 10–16
Ps. 112
or Ps. 98. 1–5
Gw Mark 12. 13–17

Ps. **106**† (or 103)
Jer. 2. 1–13
John 3. 22–end

---

9 W — **ASH WEDNESDAY**
Joel 2. 1–2, 12–17
or Isa. 58. 1–12
Ps. 51. 1–18
2 Cor. 5.20b – 6.10
Matt. 6. 1–6, 16–21
P *or* John 8. 1–11

MP: Ps. 38
Dan. 9. 3–6, 17–19
1 Tim. 6. 6–19

---

10 Th
Deut. 30. 15–end
Ps. 1
Luke 9. 22–25
P

Ps. 77
alt. Ps. 113; **115**
Jer. 2. 14–32
John 4. 1–26

---

11 F
Isa. 58. 1–9a
Ps. 51. 1–5, 17–18
Matt. 9. 14–15
P

Ps. **3**; 7
alt. Ps. 139
Jer. 3. 6–22
John 4. 27–42

---

*Chad may be celebrated with Cedd on 26 October instead of 2 March.

Second Service Evening Prayer		Calendar and Holy Communion	Morning Prayer	Evening Prayer
Ps. 89. 19–end Gen. 31. 1–24 2 Tim. 4. 9–end	Gw	**David, Bishop of Menevia, Patron of Wales, c. 601** Com. Bishop	2 Chron. 10.1 – 11.4 John 19. 17–30	Gen. 31. 1–24 2 Tim. 4. 9–end
Ps. *91*; 93 Gen. 31.25 – 32.2 Titus ch. 1	Gw	**Chad, Bishop of Lichfield, Missionary, 672** Com. Bishop	2 Chron. ch. 12 John 19. 31–end	Gen. 31.25 – 32.2 Titus ch. 1
Ps. 94 Gen. 32. 3–30 Titus ch. 2	G		2 Chron. 13.1 – 14.1 John 20. 1–10	Gen. 32. 3–30 Titus ch. 2
Ps. 102 Gen. 33. 1–17 Titus ch. 3	G		2 Chron. 14. 2–end John 20. 11–18	Gen. 33. 1–17 Titus ch. 3
Ps. 104 Gen. ch. 35 Philemon ct	G		2 Chron. 15. 1–15 John 20. 19–end	Gen. ch. 35 Philemon ct
Ps. 84 Ecclus. 48. 1–10 or 2 Kings 2. 1–12 Matt. 17. [1–8] 9–23	G	QUINQUAGESIMA Gen. 9. 8–17 Ps. 77. 11–end 1 Cor. ch. 13 Luke 18. 31–43	Ps. 72 Exod. 34. 29–end 2 Cor. 4. 3–6	Ps. 84 Ecclus. 48. 1–10 or 2 Kings 2. 1–12 Matt. 17. [1–8] 9–23
Ps. *105*† (or 103) Gen. 37. 1–11 Gal. ch. 1	Gr	**Perpetua, Martyr at Carthage, 203** Com. Martyr	Jer. ch. 1 John 3. 1–21	Gen. 37. 1–11 Gal. ch. 1
Ps. 107† Gen. 37. 12–end Gal. 2. 1–10	G		Jer. 2. 1–13 John 3. 22–end	Gen. 37. 12–end Gal. 2. 1–10
EP: Ps. *51* or Ps. 102 (or 102. 1–18) Isa. 1. 10–18 Luke 15. 11–end	P	**ASH WEDNESDAY** Ash Wed. Coll. until 23 April Commination Joel 2. 12–17 Ps. 57 James 4. 1–10 Matt. 6. 16–21	Ps. 38 Dan. 9. 3–6, 17–19 1 Tim. 6. 6–19	Ps. 51 or Ps. 102 (or 102. 1–18) Isa. 1. 10–18 Luke 15. 11–end
Ps. 74 alt. Ps. 114; *116*; 117 Gen. ch. 39 Gal. 2. 11–end	P	Exod. 24. 12–end Matt. 8. 5–13	Jer. 2. 14–32 John 4. 1–26	Gen. ch. 39 Gal. 2. 11–end
Ps. 31 alt. Ps. *130*; 131; 137 Gen. ch. 40 Gal. 3. 1–14	P	1 Kings 19. 3b–8 Matt. 5.43 – 6.6	Jer. 3. 6–22 John 4. 27–42	Gen. ch. 40 Gal. 3. 1–14

March 2011

		Sunday Principal Service Weekday Eucharist	Third Service Morning Prayer
12	Sa	Isa. 58. 9b–end Ps. 86. 1–7 Luke 5. 27–32	Ps. 71 *alt.* Ps. 120; *121*; 122 Jer. 4. 1–18 John 4. 43–end
	P		
13	S	THE FIRST SUNDAY OF LENT Gen. 2. 15–17; 3. 1–7 Ps. 32 Rom. 5. 12–19 Matt. 4. 1–11	Ps. 119. 1–16 Jer. 18. 1–11 Luke 18. 9–14
	P		
14	M	Lev. 19. 1–2, 11–18 Ps. 19. 7–end Matt. 25. 31–end	Ps. 10; *11* *alt.* Ps. 123; 124; 125; *126* Jer. 4. 19–end John 5. 1–18
	P		
15	Tu	Isa. 55. 10–11 Ps. 34. 4–6, 21–22 Matt. 6. 7–15	Ps. 44 *alt.* Ps. *132*; 133 Jer. 5. 1–19 John 5. 19–29
	P		
16	W	Ember Day* Jonah ch. 3 Ps. 51. 1–5, 17–18 Luke 11. 29–32	Ps. *6*; 17 *alt.* Ps. 119. 153–end Jer. 5. 20–end John 5. 30–end
	P		
17	Th	**Patrick, Bishop, Missionary, Patron of Ireland, *c.* 460** Com. Missionary *or* *also* Ps. 91. 1–4, 13–end Luke 10. 1–12, 17–20	Esther 14. 1–5, 12–14 *or* Isa. 55. 6–9 Ps. 138 Matt. 7. 7–12	Ps. *42*; 43 *alt.* Ps. *143*; 146 Jer. 6. 9–21 John 6. 1–15
	Pw		
18	F	*Cyril, Bishop of Jerusalem, Teacher, 386* Ember Day* Ezek. 18. 21–28 Ps. 130 Matt. 5. 20–26	Ps. 22 *alt.* Ps. 142; *144* Jer. 6. 22–end John 6. 16–27
	P		
19	Sa	JOSEPH OF NAZARETH Ember Day* 2 Sam. 7. 4–16 Ps. 89. 26–36 Rom. 4. 13–18 Matt. 1. 18–end	MP: Ps. 25; 147. 1–12 Isa. 11. 1–10 Matt. 13. 54–end
	W		
20	S	THE SECOND SUNDAY OF LENT Gen. 12. 1–4a Ps. 121 Rom. 4. 1–5, 13–17 John 3. 1–17	Ps. 74 Jer. 22. 1–9 Matt. 8. 1–13
	P		
21	M	**Thomas Cranmer, Archbishop of Canterbury, Reformation Martyr, 1556** Com. Martyr *or* Ps. 79. 8–9, 12, 14 Luke 6. 36–38	Dan. 9. 4–10	Ps. 26; *32* *alt.* Ps. *1*; 2; 3 Jer. 7. 21–end John 6. 41–51
	Pr		

*For Ember Day provision, see p. 13.

Second Service Evening Prayer		Calendar and Holy Communion	Morning Prayer	Evening Prayer
		Gregory the Great, Bishop of Rome, 604		
Ps. 73		Com. Doctor or	Jer. 4. 1–18	Gen. 41. 1–24
alt. Ps. 118		Isa. 38. 1–6a	John 4. 43–end	Gal. 3. 15–22
Gen. 41. 1–24		Mark 6. 45–end		
Gal. 3. 15–22				
ct	Pw			ct
		THE FIRST SUNDAY OF LENT		
Ps. 50. 1–15		Coll.	Ps. 119. 1–16	Ps. 50. 1–15
Deut. 6. 4–9, 16–end		(1) Lent 1	Jer. 18. 1–11	Deut. 6. 4–9, 16–end
Luke 15. 1–10		(2) Ash Wednesday	Luke 18. 9–14	Luke 15. 1–10
		Ember until 19th		
		Gen. 3. 1–6		
		Ps. 91. 1–12		
		2 Cor. 6. 1–10		
	P	Matt. 4. 1–11		
Ps. 12; *13*; 14		Ezek. 34. 11–16a	Jer. 4. 19–end	Gen. 41. 25–45
alt. Ps. *127*; 128; 129		Matt. 25. 31–end	John 5. 1–18	Gal. 3.23 – 4.7
Gen. 41. 25–45				
Gal. 3.23 – 4.7	P			
Ps. 46; *49*		Isa. 55. 6–11	Jer. 5. 1–19	Gen. 41.46 – 42.5
alt. Ps. (134); *135*		Matt. 21. 10–16	John 5. 19–29	Gal. 4. 8–20
Gen. 41.46 – 42.5				
Gal. 4. 8–20	P			
		Ember Day		
Ps. 9; *28*		Ember CEG or	Jer. 5. 20–end	Gen. 42. 6–17
alt. Ps. 136		Isa. 58. 1–9a	John 5. 30–end	Gal. 4.21 – 5.1
Gen. 42. 6–17		Matt. 12. 38–end		
Gal. 4.21 – 5.1	P			
Ps. 137; 138; *142*		Isa. 58. 9b–end	Jer. 6. 9–21	Gen. 42. 18–28
alt. Ps. *138*; 140; 141		John 8. 31–45	John 6. 1–15	Gal. 5. 2–15
Gen. 42. 18–28				
Gal. 5. 2–15	P			
		Edward, King of the W. Saxons, 978		
		Ember Day		
Ps. 54; *55*		Ember CEG or	Jer. 6. 22–end	Gen. 42. 29–end
alt. Ps. 145		Com. Martyr or	John 6. 16–27	Gal. 5. 16–end
Gen. 42. 29–end		Ezek. 18. 20–25		
Gal. 5. 16–end		John 5. 2–15		
or First EP of Joseph				
Ps. 132				
Hos. 11. 1–9				
Luke 2. 41–end				
W ct	Pr			
		To celebrate Joseph, see *Common Worship* provision.		
		Ember Day		
EP: Ps. 1; 112		Ember CEG or	Jer. 7. 1–20	Gen. 43. 1–15
Gen. 50. 22–end		Ezek. 18. 26–end	John 6. 27–40	Gal. ch. 6
Matt. 2. 13–end		Matt. 17. 1–9		
		or Luke 4. 16–21		
	P	or John 10. 1–16		ct
		THE SECOND SUNDAY OF LENT		
Ps. 135 (or 135. 1–14)		Jer. 17. 5–10	Ps. 74	Ps. 135 (or 135. 1–14)
Num. 21. 4–9		Ps. 25. 13–end	Jer. 22. 1–9	Num. 21. 4–9
Luke 14. 27–33		1 Thess. 4. 1–8	Matt. 8. 1–13	Luke 14. 27–33
	P	Matt. 15. 21–28		
		Benedict, Abbot of Monte Cassino, c. 550		
Ps. 70; *74*		Com. Abbot or	Jer. 7. 21–end	Gen. 43. 16–end
alt. Ps. 4; 7		Heb. 2. 1–10	John 6. 41–51	Heb. ch. 1
Gen. 43. 16–end		John 8. 21–30		
Heb. ch. 1	Pw			

March 2011

			Sunday Principal Service Weekday Eucharist	Third Service Morning Prayer
22	Tu		Isa. 1. 10, 16–20 Ps. 50. 8, 16–end Matt. 23. 1–12	Ps. 50 *alt.* Ps. **5**; 6; (8) Jer. 8. 1–15
	P			John 6. 52–59
23	W		Jer. 18. 18–20 Ps. 31. 4–5, 14–18 Matt. 20. 17–28	Ps. 35 *alt.* Ps. 119. 1–32 Jer. 8.18 – 9.11
	P			John 6. 60–end
24	Th	*Walter Hilton of Thurgarton, Augustinian Canon, Mystic, 1396; Oscar Romero, Archbishop of San Salvador, Martyr, 1980*		
			Jer. 17. 5–10 Ps. 1 Luke 16. 19–end	Ps. 34 *alt.* Ps. 14; **15**; 16 Jer. 9. 12–24 John 7. 1–13
	P			
25	F	**THE ANNUNCIATION OF OUR LORD TO THE BLESSED VIRGIN MARY**		
			Isa. 7. 10–14 Ps. 40. 5–11 Heb. 10. 4–10 Luke 1. 26–38	*MP:* Ps. 111; 113 1 Sam. 2. 1–10 Rom. 5. 12–end
	✠			
26	Sa	*Harriet Monsell, Founder of the Community of St John the Baptist, Clewer, 1883*		
			Mic. 7. 14–15, 18–20 Ps. 103. 1–4, 9–12 Luke 15. 1–3, 11–end	Ps. 3; **25** *alt.* Ps. 20; 21; **23** Jer. 10. 17–24 John 7. 25–36
	P			
27	S	THE THIRD SUNDAY OF LENT		
			Exod. 17. 1–7 Ps. 95 Rom. 5. 1–11 John 4. 5–42	Ps. 46 Amos 7. 10–end 2 Cor. 1. 1–11
	P			
28	M*		2 Kings 5. 1–15 Ps. 42. 1–2; 43. 1–4 Luke 4. 24–30	Ps. **5**; 7 *alt.* Ps. 27; **30** Jer. 11. 1–17
	P			John 7. 37–52
29	Tu		Song of the Three 2, 11–20 *or* Dan. 2. 20–23 Ps. 25. 3–10 Matt. 18. 21–end	Ps. 6; **9** *alt.* Ps. 32; **36** Jer. 11.18 – 12.6 John 7.53 – 8.11
	P			
30	W		Deut. 4. 1, 5–9 Ps. 147. 13–end Matt. 5. 17–19	Ps. 38 *alt.* Ps. 34 Jer. 13. 1–11
	P			John 8. 12–30
31	Th	*John Donne, Priest, Poet, 1631*		
			Jer. 7. 23–28 Ps. 95. 1–2, 6–end Luke 11. 14–23	Ps. **56**; 57 *alt.* Ps. 37† Jer. ch. 14
	P			John 8. 31–47

April 2011

1	F	*Frederick Denison Maurice, Priest, Teacher, 1872*		
			Hos. ch. 14 Ps. 81. 6–10, 13, 16 Mark 12. 28–34	Ps. 22 *alt.* Ps. 31 Jer. 15. 10–end
	P			John 8. 48–end

*The following readings may replace those provided for Holy Communion on any day during the Third Week of Lent: Exod. 17. 1–7; Ps. 95. 1–2, 6–end; John 4. 5–42.

Second Service Evening Prayer		Calendar and Holy Communion	Morning Prayer	Evening Prayer
Ps. *52*; 53; 54 *alt.* Ps. *9*; 10† Gen. 44. 1–17 Heb. 2. 1–9	P	Heb. 2. 11–end Matt. 23. 1–12	Jer. 8. 1–15 John 6. 52–59	Gen. 44. 1–17 Heb. 2. 1–9
Ps. *3*; 51 *alt.* Ps. *11*; 12; 13 Gen. 44. 18–end Heb. 2. 10–end	P	Heb. 3. 1–6 Matt. 20. 17–28	Jer. 8.18 – 9.11 John 6. 60–end	Gen. 44. 18–end Heb. 2. 10–end
First EP of The Annunciation Ps. 85 Wisd. 9. 1–12 *or* Gen. 3. 8–15 Gal. 4. 1–5 𝕎 ct	P	Heb. 3. 7–end John 5. 30–end	Jer. 9. 12–24 John 7. 1–13	*First EP of The Annunciation* Ps. 85 Wisd. 9. 1–12 *or* Gen. 3. 8–15 Gal. 4. 1–5 𝕎 ct
EP: Ps. 131; 146 Isa. 52. 1–12 Heb. 2. 5–end	𝕎	**THE ANNUNCIATION OF THE BLESSED VIRGIN MARY** Isa. 7. 10–14 [15] Ps. 113 Rom. 5. 12–19 Luke 1. 26–38	Ps. 111 1 Sam. 2. 1–10 Heb. 10. 4–10	Ps. 131; 146 Isa. 52. 1–12 Heb. 2. 5–end
Ps. *23*; 27 *alt.* Ps. *24*; 25 Gen. 46. 1–7, 28–end Heb. 4. 1–13 ct	P	Heb. ch. 5 Luke 15. 11–end	Jer. 10. 17–24 John 7. 25–36	Gen. 46. 1–7, 28–end Heb. 4. 1–13 ct
Ps. 40 Josh. 1. 1–9 Eph. 6. 10–20 *Gospel:* John 2. 13–22	P	THE THIRD SUNDAY OF LENT Num. 22. 21–31 Ps. 9. 13–end Eph. 5. 1–14 Luke 11. 14–28	Ps. 46 Amos 7. 10–end 2 Cor. 1. 1–11	Ps. 40 Josh. 1. 1–9 Eph. 6. 10–20
Ps. 11; *17* *alt.* Ps. 26; *28*; 29 Gen. 47. 1–27 Heb. 4.14 – 5.10	P	Heb. 6. 1–10 Luke 4. 23–30	Jer. 11. 1–17 John 7. 37–52	Gen. 47. 1–27 Heb. 4.14 – 5.10
Ps. 61; 62; *64* *alt.* Ps. 33 Gen. 47.28 – 48.end Heb. 5.11 – 6.12	P	Heb. 6. 11–end Matt. 18. 15–22	Jer. 11.18 – 12.6 John 7.53 – 8.11	Gen. 47.28 – 48.end Heb. 5.11 – 6.12
Ps. 36; *39* *alt.* Ps. 119. 33–56 Gen. 49. 1–32 Heb. 6. 13–end	P	Heb. 7. 1–10 Matt. 15. 1–20	Jer. 13. 1–11 John 8. 12–30	Gen. 49. 1–32 Heb. 6. 13–end
Ps. *59*; 60 *alt.* Ps. 39; *40* Gen. 49.33 – 50.end Heb. 7. 1–10	P	Heb. 7. 11–25 John 6. 26–35	Jer. ch. 14 John 8. 31–47	Gen. 49.33 – 50.end Heb. 7. 1–10
Ps. 69 *alt.* Ps. 35 Exod. 1. 1–14 Heb. 7. 11–end	P	Heb. 7. 26–end John 4. 5–26	Jer. 15. 10–end John 8. 48–end	Exod. 1. 1 14 Heb. 7. 11–end

April 2011

			Sunday Principal Service / Weekday Eucharist	Third Service / Morning Prayer

2 Sa

P

Hos. 5.15 – 6.6
Ps. 51. 1–2, 17–end
Luke 18. 9–14

Ps. 31
alt. Ps. 41; **42**; 43
Jer. 16.10 – 17.4
John 9. 1–17

---

3 S   THE FOURTH SUNDAY OF LENT
(Mothering Sunday)

1 Sam. 16. 1–13
Ps. 23
Eph. 5. 8–14
John ch. 9

Ps. 19
Isa. 43. 1–7
Eph. 2. 8–14

or, for Mothering Sunday:

P

Exod. 2. 1–10
or 1 Sam. 1. 20–end
Ps. 34. 11–20
or Ps. 127. 1–4
2 Cor. 1. 3–7
or Col. 3. 12–17
Luke 2. 33–35
or John 19. 25b–27

---

4 M*

P

Isa. 65. 17–21
Ps. 30. 1–5, 8, 11–end
John 4. 43–end

Ps. 70; **77**
alt. Ps. 44
Jer. 17. 5–18
John 9. 18–end

---

5 Tu

P

Ezek. 47. 1–9, 12
Ps. 46. 1–8
John 5. 1–3, 5–16

Ps. 54; **79**
alt. Ps. **48**; 52
Jer. 18. 1–12
John 10. 1–10

---

6 W

P

Isa. 49. 8–15
Ps. 145. 8–18
John 5. 17–30

Ps. 63; **90**
alt. Ps. 119. 57–80
Jer. 18. 13–end
John 10. 11–21

---

7 Th

P

Exod. 32. 7–14
Ps. 106. 19–23
John 5. 31–end

Ps. 53; **86**
alt. Ps. 56; **57**; (63†)
Jer. 19. 1–13
John 10. 22–end

---

8 F

P

Wisd. 2. 1, 12–22
or Jer. 26. 8–11
Ps. 34. 15–end
John 7. 1–2, 10, 25–30

Ps. 102
alt. Ps. **51**; 54
Jer. 19.14 – 20.6
John 11. 1–16

---

9 Sa   *Dietrich Bonhoeffer, Lutheran Pastor, Martyr, 1945*

P

Jer. 11. 18–20
Ps. 7. 1–2, 8–10
John 7. 40–52

Ps. 32
alt. Ps. 68
Jer. 20. 7–end
John 11. 17–27

---

10 S   THE FIFTH SUNDAY OF LENT **(Passiontide begins)**

P

Ezek. 37. 1–14
Ps. 130
Rom. 8. 6–11
John 11. 1–45

Ps. 86
Jer. 31. 27–37
John 12. 20–33

---

*The following readings may replace those provided for Holy Communion on any day during the Fourth Week of Lent: Mic. 7. 7–9; Ps. 27. 1, 9–10, 16–17; John ch. 9.

Second Service Evening Prayer	Calendar and Holy Communion	Morning Prayer	Evening Prayer
Ps. *116*; 130 *alt.* Ps. 45; *46* Exod. 1.22 – 2.10 Heb. ch. 8 ct	Heb. 8. 1–6 John 8. 1–11 P	Jer. 16.10 – 17.4 John 9. 1–17	Exod. 1.22 – 2.10 Heb. ch. 8 ct
Ps. 31. 1–8 [9–16] Mic. ch. 7 *or* Prayer of Manasseh James ch. 5 *Gospel:* John 3. 14–21 *If the Principal Service readings for The Fourth Sunday of Lent are displaced by Mothering Sunday provisions, they may be used at the Second Service.*	**THE FOURTH SUNDAY OF LENT** To celebrate Mothering Sunday, *see Common Worship* provision. Exod. 16. 2–7a Ps. 122 Gal. 4. 21–end *or* Heb. 12. 22–24 John 6. 1–14 P	Ps. 19 Isa. 43. 1–7 Eph. 2. 8–14	Ps. 31. 1–8 [9–16] Mic. ch. 7 *or* Prayer of Manasseh James ch. 5
Ps. *25*; 28 *alt.* Ps. *47*; 49 Exod. 2. 11–22 Heb. 9. 1–14	**Ambrose, Bishop of Milan, 397** Com. Doctor *or* Heb. 11. 1–6 John 2. 13–end Pw	Jer. 17. 5–18 John 9. 18–end	Exod. 2. 11–22 Heb. 9. 1–14
Ps. *80*; 82 *alt.* Ps. 50 Exod. 2.23 – 3.20 Heb. 9. 15–end	Heb. 11. 13–16a John 7. 14–24 P	Jer. 18. 1–12 John 10. 1–10	Exod. 2.23 – 3.20 Heb. 9. 15–end
Ps. 52; *91* *alt.* Ps. *59*; 60; (67) Exod. 4. 1–23 Heb. 10. 1–18	Heb. 12. 1–11 John 9. 1–17 P	Jer. 18. 13–end John 10. 11–21	Exod. 4. 1–23 Heb. 10. 1–18
Ps. 94 *alt.* Ps. 61; *62*; 64 Exod. 4.27 – 6.1 Heb. 10. 19–25	Heb. 12. 12–17 John 5. 17–27 P	Jer. 19. 1–13 John 10. 22–end	Exod. 4.27 – 6.1 Heb. 10. 19–25
Ps. 13; *16* *alt.* Ps. 38 Exod. 6. 2–13 Heb. 10. 26–end	Heb. 12. 22–end John 11. 33–46 P	Jer. 19.14 – 20.6 John 11. 1–16	Exod. 6. 2–13 Heb. 10. 26–end
Ps. *140*; 141; 142 *alt.* Ps. 65; *66* Exod. 7. 8–end Heb. 11. 1–16 ct	Heb. 13. 7–21 John 8. 12–20 P	Jer. 20. 7–end John 11. 17–27	Exod. 7. 8–end Heb. 11. 1–16 ct
Ps. 30 Lam. 3. 19–33 Matt. 20. 17–end	**THE FIFTH SUNDAY OF LENT** Exod. 24. 4–8 Ps. 143 Heb. 9. 11–15 John 8. 46–end P	Ps. 86 Jer. 31. 27–37 John 12. 20–33	Ps. 30 Lam. 3. 19–33 Matt. 20. 17–end

April 2011

			Sunday Principal Service Weekday Eucharist	Third Service Morning Prayer
11	M*	*George Augustus Selwyn, first Bishop of New Zealand, 1878*	Susanna 1–9, 15–17, 19–30, 33–62 (or 41b–62) or Josh. 2. 1–14 Ps. 23	Ps. **73**; 121 *alt.* Ps. 71 Jer. 21. 1–10 John 11. 28–44
	P		John 8. 1–11	
12	Tu		Num. 21. 4–9 Ps. 102. 1–3, 16–23 John 8. 21–30	Ps. **35**; 123 *alt.* Ps. 73 Jer. 22. 1–5, 13–19 John 11. 45–end
	P			
13	W		Dan. 3. 14–20, 24–25, 28 *Canticle:* Bless the Lord John 8. 31–42	Ps. **55**; 124 *alt.* Ps. 77 Jer. 22.20 – 23.8 John 12. 1–11
	P			
14	Th		Gen. 17. 3–9 Ps. 105. 4–9 John 8. 51–end	Ps. **40**; 125 *alt.* Ps. 78. 1–39† Jer. 23. 9–32 John 12. 12–19
	P			
15	F		Jer. 20. 10–13 Ps. 18. 1–6 John 10. 31–end	Ps. **22**; 126 *alt.* Ps. 55 Jer. ch. 24 John 12. 20–36a
	P			
16	Sa	*Isabella Gilmore, Deaconess, 1923*	Ezek. 37. 21–end *Canticle:* Jer. 31. 10–13 or Ps. 121 John 11. 45–end	Ps. **23**; 127 *alt.* Ps. **76**; 79 Jer. 25. 1–14 John 12. 36b–end
	P			
17	S	**PALM SUNDAY** *Liturgy of the Palms* Matt. 21. 1–11 Ps. 118. 1–2, 19–end (or 118. 19–24)	*Liturgy of the Passion* Isa. 50. 4–9a Ps. 31. 9–16 (or 31. 9–18) Phil. 2. 5–11 Matt. 26.14 – 27.end or Matt. 27. 11–54	Ps. 61; 62 Zech. 9. 9–12 Luke 16. 19–end
	R			
18	M	**MONDAY OF HOLY WEEK**	Isa. 42. 1–9 Ps. 36. 5–11 Heb. 9. 11–15	MP: Ps. 41 Lam. 1. 1–12a Luke 22. 1–23
	R		John 12. 1–11	
19	Tu	**TUESDAY OF HOLY WEEK**	Isa. 49. 1–7 Ps. 71. 1–14 (or 71. 1–8) 1 Cor. 1. 18–31	MP: Ps. 27 Lam. 3. 1–18 Luke 22. [24–38] 39–53
	R		John 12. 20–36	
20	W	**WEDNESDAY OF HOLY WEEK**	Isa. 50. 4–9a Ps. 70 Heb. 12. 1–3	MP: Ps. 102 (or 102. 1–18) Wisd. 1.16 – 2.1, 12–22 or Jer. 11. 18–20
	R		John 13. 21–32	Luke 22. 54–end
21	Th	**MAUNDY THURSDAY**	Exod. 12. 1–4 [5–10], 11–14 Ps. 116. 1, 10–end (or 116. 9–end) 1 Cor. 11. 23–26	MP: Ps. 42; 43 Lev. 16. 2–24 Luke 23. 1–25
	W (HC) R		John 13. 1–17, 31b–35	

*The following readings may replace those provided for Holy Communion on any day during the Fifth Week of Lent: 2 Kings 4. 18–21, 32–37; Ps. 17. 1–8, 16; John 11. 1–45.

Second Service Evening Prayer		Calendar and Holy Communion	Morning Prayer	Evening Prayer
Ps. **26**; 27 alt. Ps. **72**; 75 Exod. 8. 1–19 Heb. 11. 17–31	P	Col. 1. 13–23a John 7. 1–13	Jer. 21. 1–10 John 11. 28–44	Exod. 8. 1–19 Heb. 11. 17–31
Ps. **61**; 64 alt. Ps. 74 Exod. 8. 20–end Heb. 11.32 – 12.2	P	Col. 2. 8–12 John 7. 32–39	Jer. 22. 1–5, 13–19 John 11. 45–end	Exod. 8. 20–end Heb. 11.32 – 12.2
Ps. 56; **62** alt. Ps. 119. 81–104 Exod. 9. 1–12 Heb. 12. 3–13	P	Col. 2. 13–19 John 7. 40–end	Jer. 22.20 – 23.8 John 12. 1–11	Exod. 9. 1–12 Heb. 12. 3–13
Ps. 42; **43** alt. Ps. 78. 40–end† Exod. 9. 13–end Heb. 12. 14–end	P	Col. 3. 8–11 John 10. 22–38	Jer. 23. 9–32 John 12. 12–19	Exod. 9. 13–end Heb. 12. 14–end
Ps. 31 alt. Ps. 69 Exod. ch. 10 Heb. 13. 1–16	P	Col. 3. 12–17 John 11. 47–54	Jer. ch. 24 John 12. 20–36a	Exod. ch. 10 Heb. 13. 1–16
Ps. 128; 129; **130** alt. Ps. 81; **84** Exod. ch. 11 Heb. 13. 17–end ct	P	Col. 4. 2–6 John 6. 53–end	Jer. 25. 1–14 John 12. 36b–end	Exod. ch. 11 Heb. 13. 17–end ct
Ps. 80 Isa. 5. 1–7 Matt. 21. 33–end	R	**PALM SUNDAY** Zech. 9. 9–12 Ps. 73. 22–end Phil. 2. 5–11 Passion acc. to Matthew Matt. 27. 1–54 or Matt. 26.1 – 27.61 or Matt. 21. 1–13	Ps. 61; 62 Isa. 42. 1–9 Luke 16. 19–end	Ps. 80 Isa. 5. 1–7 Matt. 21. 33–end
EP: Ps. 25 Lam. 2. 8–19 Col. 1. 18–23	R	**MONDAY OF HOLY WEEK** Isa. 63. 1–19 Ps. 55. 1–8 Gal. 6. 1–11 Mark ch. 14	Ps. 41 Lam. 1. 1–12a John 12. 1–11	Ps. 25 Lam. 2. 8–19 Col. 1. 18–23
EP: Ps. 55. 13–24 Lam. 3. 40–51 Gal. 6. 11–end	R	**TUESDAY OF HOLY WEEK** Isa. 50. 5–11 Ps. 13 Rom. 5. 6–19 Mark 15. 1–39	Ps. 27 Lam. 3. 1–18 John 12. 20–36	Ps. 55. 13–24 Lam. 3. 40–51 Gal. 6. 11–end
EP: Ps. 88 Isa. 63. 1–9 Rev. 14.18 – 15.4	R	**WEDNESDAY OF HOLY WEEK** Isa. 49. 1–9a Ps. 54 Heb. 9. 16–end Luke ch. 22	Ps. 102 (or 102. 1–18) Wisd. 1.16 – 2.1, 12–22 or Jer. 11. 18–20 John 13. 21–32	Ps. 88 Isa. 63. 1–9 Rev. 14.18 – 15.4
EP: Ps. 39 Exod. ch. 11 Eph. 2. 11–18	**W (HC) R**	**MAUNDY THURSDAY** Exod. 12. 1–11 Ps. 43 1 Cor. 11. 17–end Luke 23. 1 49	Ps. 42; 43 Lev. 16. 2–24 John 13. 1–17, 31b–35	Ps. 39 Exod. ch. 11 Eph. 2. 11–18

April 2011

			Sunday Principal Service Weekday Eucharist	Third Service Morning Prayer
22	F R	**GOOD FRIDAY**	Isa. 52.13 – 53.end Ps. 22 (or 22. 1–11 or 22. 1–21) Heb. 10. 16–25 or Heb. 4. 14–16; 5. 7–9 John 18.1 – 19.end	*MP*: Ps. 69 Gen. 22. 1–18 A part of John 18 – 19 if not read at the Principal Service or Heb. 10. 1–10
23	Sa	**Easter Eve** (George transferred to 2 May) *These readings are for use at* *services other than the Easter Vigil*	Job 14. 1–14 or Lam. 3. 1–9, 19–24 Ps. 31. 1–4, 15–16 (or 31. 1–5) 1 Pet. 4. 1–8 Matt. 27. 57–end or John 19. 38–end	Ps. 142 Hos. 6. 1–6 John 2. 18–22
24	S ƷƷƷ	**EASTER DAY** *The following readings and psalms* *(or canticles) are provided for use at* *the Easter Vigil. A minimum of three* *Old Testament readings should be* *chosen. The reading from* Exodus *ch. 14 should always be used.*	Gen. 1.1 – 2.4a & Ps. 136. 1–9, 23–end Gen. 7. 1–5, 11–18; 8. 6–18; 9. 8–13 & Ps. 46 Gen. 22. 1–18 & Ps. 16 Exod. 14. 10–end; 15. 20–21 & *Canticle*: Exod. 15. 1b–13, 17–18 Isa. 55. 1–11 & *Canticle*: Isa. 12. 2–end Baruch 3.9–15, 32 – 4.4 & Ps. 19 or Prov. 8. 1–8, 19–21; 9. 4b–6 & Ps. 19 Ezek. 36. 24–28 & Ps. 42; 43 Ezek. 37. 1–14 & Ps. 143 Zeph. 3. 14–end & Ps. 98 Rom. 6. 3–11 & Ps. 114 Matt. 28. 1–10	
	ƷƷƷ	*Easter Day Services* *The reading from Acts must be* *used as either the first or second* *reading at the Principal Service.*	Acts 10. 34–43 or Jer. 31. 1–6 Ps. 118. 1–2, 14–24 (or 118. 14–24) Col. 3. 1–4 or Acts 10. 34–43 John 20. 1–18 or Matt. 28. 1–10	*MP*: Ps. 114; 117 Exod. 14.10–18, 26 – 15.2 Rev. 15. 2–4
25	M W	MONDAY OF EASTER WEEK (Mark transferred to 3 May)	Acts 2. 14, 22–32 Ps. 16. 1–2, 6–end Matt. 28. 8–15	Ps. *111*; 117; 146 Song of Sol. 1.9 – 2.7 Mark 16. 1–8
26	Tu W	TUESDAY OF EASTER WEEK	Acts 2. 36–41 Ps. 33. 4–5, 18–end John 20. 11–18	Ps. *112*; 147. 1–12 Song of Sol. 2. 8–end Luke 24. 1–12
27	W W	WEDNESDAY OF EASTER WEEK	Acts 3. 1–10 Ps. 105. 1–9 Luke 24. 13–35	Ps. *113*; 147. 13–end Song of Sol. ch. 3 Matt. 28. 16–end
28	Th W	THURSDAY OF EASTER WEEK	Acts 3. 11–end Ps. 8 Luke 24. 35–48	Ps. *114*; 148 Song of Sol. 5.2 – 6.3 Luke 7. 11–17
29	F W	FRIDAY OF EASTER WEEK	Acts 4. 1–12 Ps. 118. 1–4, 22–26 John 21. 1–14	Ps. *115*; 149 Song of Sol. 7.10 – 8.4 Luke 8. 41–end

Second Service Evening Prayer		Calendar and Holy Communion	Morning Prayer	Evening Prayer
EP: Ps. 130; 143 Lam. 5. 15–end A part of John 18 – 19 if not read at the Principal Service, especially John 19. 38–end or Col. 1. 18–23	**R**	**GOOD FRIDAY** Alt. Collect Passion acc. to John Alt. Gospel, if Passion is read Num. 21. 4–9 Ps. 140. 1–9 Heb. 10. 1–25 John 19. 1–37 or John 19. 38–end	Ps. 69 Gen. 22. 1–18 John ch. 18	Ps. 130; 143 Lam. 5. 15–end John 19. 38–end
Ps. 116 Job 19. 21–27 1 John 5. 5–12		**Easter Eve** Job 14. 1–14 1 Pet. 3. 17–22 Matt. 27. 57–end	Ps. 142 Hos. 6. 1–6 John 2. 18–22	Ps. 116 Job 19. 21–27 1 John 5. 5–12
		EASTER DAY Exod. 12. 21–28 Ps. 111 Col. 3. 1–7 John 20. 1–10	Ps. 114; 117 Exod. 14.10–18, 26 – 15.2 Rev. 15. 2–4	Ps. 105 or Ps. 66. 1–11 Song of Sol. 3. 2–5; 8. 6–7 John 20. 11–18 or Rev. 1. 12–18
EP: Ps. 105 or Ps. 66. 1–11 Song of Sol. 3. 2–5; 8. 6–7 John 20. 11–18 *if not used at the Principal Service* or Rev. 1. 12–18	𝍦			
Ps. 135 Exod. 12. 1–14 1 Cor. 15. 1–11	**W**	**MONDAY OF EASTER WEEK** (Mark transferred to 3 May) Hos. 6. 1–6 Easter Anthems Acts 10. 34–43 Luke 24. 13–35	Song of Sol. 1.9 – 2.7 Mark 16. 1–8	Exod. 12. 1–14 1 Cor. 15. 1–11
Ps. 136 Exod. 12. 14–36 1 Cor. 15. 12–19	**W**	**TUESDAY OF EASTER WEEK** 1 Kings 17. 17–end Ps. 16. 9–end Acts 13. 26–41 Luke 24. 36b–48	Song of Sol. 2. 8–end Luke 24. 1–12	Exod. 12. 14–36 1 Cor. 15. 12–19
Ps. 105 Exod. 12. 37–end 1 Cor. 15. 20–28	**W**	**WEDNESDAY OF EASTER WEEK** Isa. 42. 10–16 Ps. 111 Acts 3. 12–18 John 20. 11–18	Song of Sol. ch. 3 Matt. 28. 16–end	Exod. 12. 37–end 1 Cor. 15. 20–28
Ps. 106 Exod. 13. 1–16 1 Cor. 15. 29–34	**W**	**THURSDAY OF EASTER WEEK** Isa. 43. 16–21 Ps. 113 Acts 8. 26–end John 21. 1–14	Song of Sol. 5.2 – 6.3 Luke 7. 11–17	Exod. 13. 1–16 1 Cor. 15. 29–34
Ps. 107 Exod. 13.17 – 14.14 1 Cor. 15. 35–50	**W**	**FRIDAY OF EASTER WEEK** Ezek. 37. 1–14 Ps. 116. 1–9 1 Pet. 3. 18–end Matt. 28. 16–end	Song of Sol. 7.10 – 8.4 Luke 8. 41–end	Exod. 13.17 – 14.14 1 Cor. 15. 35–50

April 2011

			Sunday Principal Service Weekday Eucharist	Third Service Morning Prayer
30	Sa	SATURDAY OF EASTER WEEK	Acts 4. 13–21 Ps. 118. 1–4, 14–21 Mark 16. 9–15	Ps. *116*; 150 Song of Sol. 8. 5–7 John 11. 17–44
	W			

May 2011

1	S	THE SECOND SUNDAY OF EASTER (Philip and James transferred to 4 May) *The reading from Acts must be* *used as either the first or second* *reading at the Principal Service.*	Acts 2. 14a, 22–32 [or Exod. 14. 10–end; 15. 20–21] Ps. 16 1 Pet. 1. 3–9 John 20. 19–end	Ps. 81. 1–10 Exod. 12. 1–17 1 Cor. 5. 6b–8
	W			
2	M	GEORGE, MARTYR, PATRON OF ENGLAND, c. 304 (transferred from 23 April)	1 Macc. 2. 59–64 or Rev. 12. 7–12 Ps. 126 2 Tim. 2. 3–13 John 15. 18–21	MP: Ps. 5; 146 Josh. 1. 1–9 Eph. 6. 10–20
	R			
3	Tu	MARK THE EVANGELIST (transferred from 25 April)	Prov. 15. 28–end or Acts 15. 35–end Ps. 119. 9–16 Eph. 4. 7–16 Mark 13. 5–13	MP: Ps. 37. 23–end; 148 Isa. 62. 6–10 or Ecclus. 51. 13–end Acts 12.25 – 13.13
	R			
4	W	PHILIP AND JAMES, APOSTLES (transferred from 1 May)	Isa. 30. 15–21 Ps. 119. 1–8 Eph. 1. 3–10 John 14. 1–14	MP: Ps. 139; 146 Prov. 4. 10–18 James 1. 1–12
	R			
5	Th		Acts 5. 27–33 Ps. 34. 1, 15–end John 3. 31–end	Ps. *28*; 29 alt. Ps. 14; *15*; 16 Deut. 4. 1–14 John 21. 1–14
	W			
6	F		Acts 5. 34–42 Ps. 27. 1–5, 16–17 John 6. 1–15	Ps. 57; *61* alt. Ps. 17; *19* Deut. 4. 15–31 John 21. 15–19
	W			
7	Sa		Acts 6. 1–7 Ps. 33. 1–5, 18–19 John 6. 16–21	Ps. 63; *84* alt. Ps. 20; 21; *23* Deut. 4. 32–40 John 21. 20–end
	W			
8	S	THE THIRD SUNDAY OF EASTER *The reading from Acts must be* *used as either the first or second* *reading at the Principal Service.*	Acts 2. 14a, 36–41 [or Zeph. 3. 14–end] Ps. 116. 1–3, 10–end (or 116. 1–7) 1 Pet. 1. 17–23 Luke 24. 13–35	Ps. 23 Isa. 40. 1–11 1 Pet. 5. 1–11
	W			

Second Service Evening Prayer		Calendar and Holy Communion	Morning Prayer	Evening Prayer
		SATURDAY OF EASTER WEEK		
Ps. 145		Zech. 8. 1–8	Song of Sol. 8. 5–7	Exod. 14. 15–end
Exod. 14. 15–end		Ps. 118. 14–21	John 11. 17–44	1 Cor. 15. 51–end
1 Cor. 15. 51–end		1 Pet. 2. 1–10		
ct	W	John 20. 24–end		ct
		THE FIRST SUNDAY AFTER EASTER		
		(Philip and James transferred to 4 May)		
Ps. 30. 1–5		Ezek. 37. 1–10	Ps. 81. 1–10	Ps. 30. 1–5
Dan. 6. [1–5] 6–23		Ps. 81. 1–4	Exod. 12. 1–17	Dan. 6. [1–5] 6–23
Mark 15. 46 – 16. 8		1 John 5. 4–12	1 Cor. 5. 6b–8	Mark 15. 46 – 16. 8
or First EP of George		John 20. 19–23		
Ps. 111; 116				
Jer. 15. 15–end				
Heb. 11. 32 – 12. 2				
R ct	W			
EP: Ps. 3; 11			Deut. 1. 3–18	Exod. 15. 1–21
Isa. 43. 1–7			John 20. 1–10	Col. 1. 1–14
John 15. 1–8				*or First EP of Mark*
or First EP of Mark				(Ps. 19)
Ps. 19				Isa. 52. 7–10
Isa. 52. 7–10				Mark 1. 1–15
Mark 1. 1–15				
ct	W			**R** ct
		MARK THE EVANGELIST		
		(transferred from 25 April)		
EP: Ps. 45		Prov. 15. 28–end	(Ps. 37. 23–end; 148)	(Ps. 45)
Ezek. 1. 4–14		Ps. 119. 9–16	Isa. 62. 6–10	Ezek. 1. 4–14
2 Tim. 4. 1–11		Eph. 4. 7–16	*or Ecclus.* 51. 13–end	2 Tim. 4. 1–11
or First EP of Philip and		John 15. 1–11	Acts 12.25 – 13.13	*or First EP of Philip*
James				*and James*
Ps. 25				(Ps. 119. 1–8)
Isa. 40. 27–end				Isa. 40. 27–end
John 12. 20–26				John 12. 20–26
ct	R			ct
		PHILIP AND JAMES, APOSTLES		
		(transferred from 1 May)		
EP: Ps. 149		Prov. 4. 10–18	(Ps. 139; 146)	(Ps. 149)
Job 23. 1–12		Ps. 25. 1–9	Isa. 30. 1–5	Job 23. 1–12
John 1. 43–end		James 1. [1] 2–12	John 12. 20–26	John 1. 43–end
	R	John 14. 1–14		
Ps. 34			Deut. 4. 1–14	Exod. ch. 17
alt. Ps. 18†			John 21. 1–14	Col. 2.16 – 3.11
Exod. ch. 17				
Col. 2.16 – 3.11	W			
		John the Evangelist, ante Portam Latinam		
Ps. 118		CEG of 27 December	Deut. 4. 15–31	Exod. 18. 1–12
alt. Ps. 22			John 21. 15–19	Col. 3.12 – 4.1
Exod. 18. 1–12				
Col. 3.12 – 4.1	W			
Ps. 66			Deut. 4. 32–40	Exod. 18. 13–end
alt. Ps. **24**; 25			John 21. 20–end	Col. 4. 2–end
Exod. 18. 13–end				
Col. 4. 2–end				
ct	W			ct
		THE SECOND SUNDAY AFTER EASTER		
Ps. 48		Ezek. 34. 11–16a	Ps. 23	Ps. 48
Hag. 1.13 – 2.9		Ps. 23	Isa. 40. 1–11	Hag. 1.13 – 2.9
1 Cor. 3. 10–17		1 Pet. 2. 19–end	1 Pet. 5. 1–11	1 Cor. 3. 10–17
Gospel: John 2. 13–22		John 10. 11–16		
	W			

May 2011

			Sunday Principal Service / Weekday Eucharist	Third Service / Morning Prayer
9	M		Acts 6. 8–15 Ps. 119. 17–24 John 6. 22–29	Ps. **96**; 97 alt. Ps. 27; **30** Deut. 5. 1–22
	W			Eph. 1. 1–14
10	Tu		Acts 7.51 – 8.1a Ps. 31. 1–5, 16 John 6. 30–35	Ps. **98**; 99; 100 alt. Ps. 32; **36** Deut. 5. 22–end
	W			Eph. 1. 15–end
11	W		Acts 8. 1b–8 Ps. 66. 1–6 John 6. 35–40	Ps. 105 alt. Ps. 34 Deut. ch. 6
	W			Eph. 2. 1–10
12	Th		Acts 8. 26–end Ps. 66. 7–8, 14–end John 6. 44–51	Ps. 136 alt. Ps. 37† Deut. 7. 1–11
	W			Eph. 2. 11–end
13	F		Acts 9. 1–20 Ps. 117 John 6. 52–59	Ps. 107 alt. Ps. 31 Deut. 7. 12–end Eph. 3. 1–13
	W			
14	Sa	**MATTHIAS THE APOSTLE***	Isa. 22. 15–end or Acts 1. 15–end Ps. 15 Acts 1. 15–end or 1 Cor. 4. 1–7 John 15. 9–17	MP: Ps. 16; 147. 1–12 1 Sam. 2. 27–35 Acts 2. 37–end
	R	or, if Matthias is celebrated on 24 February:	Acts 9. 31–42 Ps. 116. 10–15 John 6. 60–69	Ps. 108; **110**; 111 alt. Ps. 41; **42**; 43 Deut. ch. 8 Eph. 3. 14–end
	W			
15	S	**THE FOURTH SUNDAY OF EASTER** The reading from Acts must be used as either the first or second reading at the Principal Service.	Acts 2. 42–end [or Gen. ch. 7] Ps. 23 1 Pet. 2. 19–end	Ps. 106. 6–24 Neh. 9. 6–15 1 Cor. 10. 1–13
	W		John 10. 1–10	
16	M	Caroline Chisholm, Social Reformer, 1877	Acts 11. 1–18 Ps. 42. 1–2; 43. 1–4 John 10. 1–10 (or 11–18)	Ps. 103 alt. Ps. 44 Deut. 9. 1–21
	W			Eph. 4. 1–16
17	Tu		Acts 11. 19–26 Ps. 87 John 10. 22–30	Ps. 139 alt. Ps. **48**; 52 Deut. 9.23 – 10.5
	W			Eph. 4. 17–end
18	W		Acts 12.24 – 13.5 Ps. 67 John 12. 44–end	Ps. 135 alt. Ps. 119. 57–80 Deut. 10. 12–end
	W			Eph. 5. 1–14
19	Th	**Dunstan, Archbishop of Canterbury, Restorer of Monastic Life, 988** Com. Bishop or esp. Matt. 24. 42–46 also Exod. 31. 1–5	Acts 13. 13–25 Ps. 89. 1–2, 20–26 John 13. 16–20	Ps. 118 alt. Ps. 56; **57**; (63†) Deut. 11. 8–end
	W			Eph. 5. 15–end

*Matthias may be celebrated on 24 February instead of 14 May.

Second Service Evening Prayer	Calendar and Holy Communion	Morning Prayer	Evening Prayer
Ps. *61*; 65 *alt.* Ps. 26; *28*; 29 Exod. ch. 19 Luke 1. 1–25 W		Deut. 5. 1–22 Eph. 1. 1–14	Exod. ch. 19 Luke 1. 1–25
Ps. 71 *alt.* Ps. 33 Exod. 20. 1–21 Luke 1. 26–38 W		Deut. 5. 22–end Eph. 1. 15–end	Exod. 20. 1–21 Luke 1. 26–38
Ps. 67; *72* *alt.* Ps. 119. 33–56 Exod. ch. 24 Luke 1. 39–56 W		Deut. ch. 6 Eph. 2. 1–10	Exod. ch. 24 Luke 1. 39–56
Ps. 73 *alt.* Ps. 39; *40* Exod. 25. 1–22 Luke 1. 57–end W		Deut. 7. 1–11 Eph. 2. 11–end	Exod. 25. 1–22 Luke 1. 57–end
Ps. 77 *alt.* Ps. 35 Exod. 28. 1–4a, 29–38 Luke 2. 1–20 *or First EP of Matthias* Ps. 147 Isa. 22. 15–22 Phil. 3.13b – 4.1 **R ct** W		Deut. 7. 12–end Eph. 3. 1–13	Exod. 28. 1–4a, 29–38 Luke 2. 1–20
EP: Ps. 80 1 Sam. 16. 1–13a Matt. 7. 15–27		Deut. ch. 8 Eph. 3. 14–end	Exod. 29. 1–9 Luke 2. 21–40
Ps. 23; *27* *alt.* Ps. 45; *46* Exod. 29. 1–9 Luke 2. 21–40 ct W			ct
Ps. 29. 1–10 Ezra 3. 1–13 Eph. 2. 11–end *Gospel:* Luke 19. 37–end W	**THE THIRD SUNDAY AFTER EASTER** Gen. 45. 3–10 Ps. 57 1 Pet. 2. 11–17 John 16. 16–22	Ps. 106. 6–24 Neh. 9. 6–15 1 Cor. 10. 1–13	Ps. 29. 1–10 Ezra 3. 1–13 Eph. 2. 11–end
Ps. 112; 113; *114* *alt.* Ps. *47*; 49 Exod. 32. 1–14 Luke 2. 41–end W		Deut. 9. 1–21 Eph. 4. 1–16	Exod. 32. 1–14 Luke 2. 41–end
Ps. 115; *116* *alt.* Ps. 50 Exod. 32. 15–34 Luke 3. 1–14 W		Deut. 9.23 – 10.5 Eph. 4. 17–end	Exod. 32. 15–34 Luke 3. 1–14
Ps. *47*; 48 *alt.* Ps. *59*; 60; (67) Exod. ch. 33 Luke 3. 15–22 W		Deut. 10. 12–end Eph. 5. 1–14	Exod. ch. 33 Luke 3. 15–22
Ps. 81; *85* *alt.* Ps. 61; *62*; 64 Exod. 34. 1–10, 27–end Luke 4. 1–13 W	**Dunstan, Archbishop of Canterbury, Restorer of Monastic Life, 988** Com. Bishop	Deut. 11. 8–end Eph. 5. 15–end	Exod. 34. 1–10, 27–end Luke 4. 1–13

May 2011

		Sunday Principal Service Weekday Eucharist		Third Service Morning Prayer

20 F

Alcuin of York, Deacon, Abbot of Tours, 804
Com. Religious   *or*   Acts 13. 26–33   Ps. 33
also Col. 3. 12–16   Ps. 2   *alt*. Ps. *51*; 54
John 4. 19–24   John 14. 1–6   Deut. 12. 1–14

W   Eph. 6. 1–9

21 Sa

Helena, Protector of the Holy Places, 330
                                   Acts 13. 44–end   Ps. 34
                                     Ps. 98. 1–5   *alt*. Ps. 68
                                     John 14. 7–14   Deut. 15. 1–18

W   Eph. 6. 10–end

22 S

THE FIFTH SUNDAY OF EASTER
The reading from Acts must be   Acts 7. 55–end   Ps. 30
used as either the first or second   [or Gen. 8. 1–19]   Ezek. 37. 1–12
reading at the Principal Service.   Ps. 31. 1–5, 15–16 (or 31. 1–5)   John 5. 19–29
                                     1 Pet. 2. 2–10

W   John 14. 1–14

23 M

                                     Acts 14. 5–18   Ps. 145
                                     Ps. 118. 1–3, 14–15   *alt*. Ps. 71
                                     John 14. 21–26   Deut. 16. 1–20

W   1 Pet. 1. 1–12

24 Tu

John and Charles Wesley, Evangelists, Hymn Writers, 1791 and 1788
Com. Pastor   *or*   Acts 14. 19–end   Ps. *19*; 147. 1–12
also Eph. 5. 15–20   Ps. 145. 10–end   *alt*. Ps. 73
                                     John 14. 27–end   Deut. 17. 8–end

W   1 Pet. 1. 13–end

25 W

The Venerable Bede, Monk at Jarrow, Scholar, Historian, 735
Aldhelm, Bishop of Sherborne, 709
Com. Religious   *or*   Acts 15. 1–6   Ps. *30*; 147. 13–end
also Ecclus. 39. 1–10   Ps. 122. 1–5   *alt*. Ps. 77
                                     John 15. 1–8   Deut. 18. 9–end

W   1 Pet. 2. 1–10

26 Th

Augustine, first Archbishop of Canterbury, 605
John Calvin, Reformer, 1564; Philip Neri, Founder of the Oratorians, Spiritual Guide, 1595
Com. Bishop   *or*   Acts 15. 7–21   Ps. *57*; 148
also 1 Thess. 2. 2b–8   Ps. 96. 1–3, 7–10   *alt*. Ps. 78. 1–39†
Matt. 13. 31–33   John 15. 9–11   Deut. ch. 19

W   1 Pet. 2. 11–end

27 F

                                     Acts 15. 22–31   Ps. *138*; 149
                                     Ps. 57. 8–end   *alt*. Ps. 55
                                     John 15. 12–17   Deut. 21.22 – 22.8

W   1 Pet. 3. 1–12

28 Sa

Lanfranc, Prior of Le Bec, Archbishop of Canterbury, Scholar, 1089
                                     Acts 16. 1–10   Ps. *146*; 150
                                     Ps. 100   *alt*. Ps. *76*; 79
                                     John 15. 18–21   Deut. 24. 5–end

W   1 Pet. 3. 13–end

29 S

THE SIXTH SUNDAY OF EASTER

The reading from Acts must be   Acts 17. 22–31   Ps. 73. 21–28
used as either the first or second   [or Gen. 8.20 – 9.17]   Job 14. 1–2, 7–15;
reading at the Principal Service.   Ps. 66. 7–18   19. 23–27a
                                     1 Pet. 3. 13–end   1 Thess. 4. 13–end

W   John 14. 15–21

Second Service Evening Prayer		Calendar and Holy Communion	Morning Prayer	Evening Prayer
Ps. 36; 40 alt. Ps. 38 Exod. 35.20 – 36.7 Luke 4. 14–30	W		Deut. 12. 1–14 Eph. 6. 1–9	Exod. 35.20 – 36.7 Luke 4. 14–30
Ps. 84; 86 alt. Ps. 65; 66 Exod. 40. 17–end Luke 4. 31–37 ct	W		Deut. 15. 1–18 Eph. 6. 10–end	Exod. 40. 17–end Luke 4. 31–37 ct
Ps. 147. 1–12 Zech. 4. 1–10 Rev. 21. 1–14 Gospel: Luke 2. 25–32 [33–38]	W	**THE FOURTH SUNDAY AFTER EASTER** Job 19. 21–27a Ps. 66. 14–end James 1. 17–21 John 16. 5–15	Ps. 30 Ezek. 37. 1–12 John 5. 19–29	Ps. 147. 1–12 Zech. 4. 1–10 Rev. 21. 1–14
Ps. 105 alt. Ps. 72; 75 Num. 9. 15–end; 10. 33–end Luke 4. 38–end	W		Deut. 16. 1–20 1 Pet. 1. 1–12	Num. 9. 15–end; 10. 33–end Luke 4. 38–end
Ps. 96; 97 alt. Ps. 74 Num. 11. 1–33 Luke 5. 1–11	W		Deut. 17. 8–end 1 Pet. 1. 13–end	Num. 11. 1–33 Luke 5. 1–11
Ps. 98; 99; 100 alt. Ps. 119. 81–104 Num. ch. 12 Luke 5. 12–26	W		Deut. 18. 9–end 1 Pet. 2. 1–10	Num. ch. 12 Luke 5. 12–26
Ps. 104 alt. Ps. 78. 40–end† Num. 13. 1–3, 17–end Luke 5. 27–end	W	**Augustine, first Archbishop of Canterbury, 605** Com. Bishop	Deut. ch. 19 1 Pet. 2. 11–end	Num. 13. 1–3, 17–end Luke 5. 27–end
Ps. 66 alt. Ps. 69 Num. 14. 1–25 Luke 6. 1–11	W	**The Venerable Bede, Monk at Jarrow, Scholar, Historian, 735** Com. Religious	Deut. 21.22 – 22.8 1 Pet. 3. 1–12	Num. 14. 1–25 Luke 6. 1–11
Ps. 118 alt. Ps. 81; 84 Num. 14. 26–end Luke 6. 12–26 ct	W		Deut. 24. 5–end 1 Pet. 3. 13–end	Num. 14. 26–end Luke 6. 12–26 ct
Ps. 87; 36. 5–10 Zech. 8. 1–13 Rev. 21.22 – 22.5 Gospel: John 21. 1–14	W	**THE FIFTH SUNDAY AFTER EASTER** Rogation Sunday Joel 2. 21–26 Ps. 66. 1–8 James 1. 22–end John 16. 23b–end	Ps. 73. 21–28 Job 14. 1–2, 7–15; 19. 23–27a 1 Thess. 4. 13–end	Ps. 87; 36. 5–10 Zech. 8. 1–13 Rev. 21.22 – 22.5

May 2011

				Sunday Principal Service Weekday Eucharist	Third Service Morning Prayer

30 M **Josephine Butler, Social Reformer, 1906**
Joan of Arc, Visionary, 1431; Apolo Kivebulaya, Evangelist in Central Africa, 1933
Rogation Day**

Com. Saint	*or*	Acts 16. 11–15	Ps. **65**; 67
esp. Isa. 58. 6–11		Ps. 149. 1–5	*alt.* Ps. **80**; 82
also 1 John 3. 18–23		John 15.26 – 16.4	Deut. ch. 26
Matt. 9. 10–13			1 Pet. 4. 1–11

W

31 Tu THE VISIT OF THE BLESSED VIRGIN MARY TO ELIZABETH*
Rogation Day**

Zeph. 3. 14–18	*MP:* Ps. 85; 150
Ps. 113	1 Sam. 2. 1–10
Rom. 12. 9–16	Mark 3. 31–end
W	Luke 1. 39–49 [50–56]

or, if The Visitation is celebrated on 2 July:

Acts 16. 22–34	Ps. 124; 125; **126**; 127
Ps. 138	*alt.* Ps. 87; **89**. **1–18**
John 16. 5–11	Deut. 28. 1–14
W	1 Pet. 4. 12–end

June 2011

1 W **Justin, Martyr at Rome, c. 165**
Rogation Day**

Com. Martyr	*or*	Acts 17.15, 22 – 18.1	Ps. **132**; 133
esp. John 15. 18–21		Ps. 148. 1–2, 11–end	*alt.* Ps. 119. 105–128
also 1 Macc. 2. 15–22		John 16. 12–15	Deut. 28. 58–end
1 Cor. 1. 18–25			1 Pet. ch. 5

Wr

2 Th **ASCENSION DAY**
*The reading from Acts must be
used as either the first or second
reading at the Eucharist.*

Acts 1. 1–11	*MP:* Ps. 110; 150
or Dan. 7. 9–14	Isa. 52. 7–end
Ps. 47 or Ps. 93	Heb. 7. [11–25] 26–end
Eph. 1. 15–end	
or Acts 1. 1–11	
Luke 24. 44–end	

3 F *The Martyrs of Uganda, 1885–87 and 1977*

Acts 18. 9–18	Ps. 20; **81**
Ps. 47. 1–6	*alt.* Ps. **88**; (95)
John 16. 20–23	Deut. 29. 2–15
	1 John 1.1 – 2.6
W	[Exod. 35.30 – 36.1
	Gal. 5. 13–end]***

4 Sa *Petroc, Abbot of Padstow, 6th century*

Acts 18. 22–end	Ps. 21; **47**
Ps. 47. 1–2, 7–end	*alt.* Ps. 96; **97**; 100
John 16. 23–28	Deut. ch. 30
	1 John 2. 7–17
	[Num. 11. 16–17, 24–29
W	1 Cor. ch. 2]

5 S THE SEVENTH SUNDAY OF EASTER (SUNDAY AFTER ASCENSION DAY)
*The reading from Acts must be
used as either the first or second
reading at the Principal Service.*

Acts 1. 6–14	Ps. 104. 26–35
[or Ezek. 36. 24–28]	Isa. 65. 17–end
Ps. 68. 1–10, 32–35	Rev. 21. 1–8
(or 68. 1–10)	
1 Pet. 4. 12–14; 5. 6–11	
W	John 17. 1–11

*The Visit of the Blessed Virgin Mary to Elizabeth may be celebrated on 2 July instead of 31 May.
**For Rogation Day provision, see p. 12.
***The alternative readings in square brackets may be used at one of the offices, in preparation for the Day of Pentecost.

Second Service Evening Prayer	Calendar and Holy Communion		Morning Prayer	Evening Prayer
Ps. *121*; 122; 123 alt. Ps. *85*; 86 Num. 16. 1–35 Luke 6. 27–38 or First EP of the Visit of Mary to Elizabeth Ps. 45 Song of Sol. 2. 8–14 Luke 1. 26–38 ct	Rogation Day Job 28. 1–11 Ps. 107. 1–9 James 5. 7–11 Luke 6. 36–42	W	Deut. ch. 26 1 Pet. 4. 1–11	Num. 16. 1–35 Luke 6. 27–38
EP: Ps. 122; 127; 128 Zech. 2. 10–end John 3. 25–30	Rogation Day Deut. 8. 1–10 Ps. 121 James 5. 16–end Luke 11. 5–13		Deut. 28. 1–14 1 Pet. 4. 12–end	Num. 16. 36–end Luke 6. 39–end
Ps. *128*; 129; 130; 131 alt. Ps. 89. 19–end Num. 16. 36–end Luke 6. 39–end		W		
First EP of Ascension Day Ps. 15; 24 2 Sam. 23. 1–5 Col. 2.20 – 3.4 ℣ ct	**Nicomede, Priest and Martyr at Rome (date unknown)** Rogation Day Com. Martyr or Deut. 31. 1–7 Ps. 108. 1–6 Eph. 4. 7–13 John 17. 1–11	Wr	Deut. 28. 58–end 1 Pet. ch. 5	First EP of Ascension Day Ps. 15; 24 2 Sam. 23. 1–5 Col. 2.20 – 3.4 ℣ ct
EP: Ps. 8 Song of the Three 29–37 or 2 Kings 2. 1–15 Rev. ch. 5 Gospel: Mark 16. 14–end	**ASCENSION DAY** Dan. 7. 13–14 Ps. 68. 1–6 Acts 1. 1–11 Mark 16. 14–end or Luke 24. 44–end	℣	Ps. 110; 150 Isa. 52. 7–end Heb. 7. [11–25] 26–end	Ps. 8 Song of the Three 29–37 or 2 Kings 2. 1–15 Rev. ch. 5
Ps. 145 alt. Ps. 102 Num. 20. 1–13 Luke 7. 11–17	Ascension CEG	W	Deut. 29. 2–15 1 John 1.1 – 2.6 [Exod. 35.30 – 36.1 Gal. 5. 13–end]***	Num. 20. 1–13 Luke 7. 11–17
Ps. 84; *85* alt. Ps. 104 Num. 21. 4–9 Luke 7. 18–35 ct	Ascension CEG	W	Deut. ch. 30 1 John 2. 7–17 [Num. 11. 16–17, 24–29 1 Cor. ch. 2]	Num. 21. 4–9 Luke 7. 18–35 ct
Ps. 47 2 Sam. 23. 1–5 Eph. 1. 15–end Gospel: Mark 16. 14–end	**THE SUNDAY AFTER ASCENSION DAY** 2 Kings 2. 9–15 Ps. 68. 32–end 1 Pet. 4. 7–11 John 15.26 – 16.4a	W	Ps. 104. 26–35 Isa. 65. 17–end Rev. 21. 1–8	Ps. 47 2 Sam. 23. 1–5 Eph. 1. 15–end

June 2011

			Sunday Principal Service Weekday Eucharist	Third Service Morning Prayer
6	M	*Ini Kopuria, Founder of the Melanesian Brotherhood, 1945*	Acts 19. 1–8 Ps. 68. 1–6 John 16. 29–end	Ps. *93*; 96; 97 *alt.* Ps. *98*; 99; 101 Deut. 31. 1–13 1 John 2. 18–end
	W			[Num. 27. 15–end 1 Cor. ch. 3]
7	Tu		Acts 20. 17–27 Ps. 68. 9–10, 18–19 John 17. 1–11	Ps. 98; *99*; 100 *alt.* Ps. *106*† (or 103) Deut. 31. 14–29 1 John 3. 1–10
	W			[1 Sam. 10. 1–10 1 Cor. 12. 1–13]
8	W	**Thomas Ken, Bishop of Bath and Wells, Nonjuror, Hymn Writer, 1711** Com. Bishop *or* *esp.* 2 Cor. 4. 1–10 Matt. 24. 42–46	Acts 20. 28–end Ps. 68. 27–28, 32–end John 17. 11–19	Ps. 2; *29* *alt.* Ps. 110; *111*; 112 Deut. 31.30 – 32.14 1 John 3. 11–end
	W			[1 Kings 19. 1–18 Matt. 3. 13–end]
9	Th	**Columba, Abbot of Iona, Missionary, 597** *Ephrem of Syria, Deacon, Hymn Writer, Teacher, 373* Com. Missionary *or* *also* Titus 2. 11–end	Acts 22. 30; 23. 6–11 Ps. 16. 1, 5–end John 17. 20–end	Ps. *24*; 72 *alt.* Ps. 113; *115* Deut. 32. 15–47 1 John 4. 1–6
	W			[Ezek. 11. 14–20 Matt. 9.35 – 10.20]
10	F		Acts 25. 13–21 Ps. 103. 1–2, 11–12, 19–20 John 21. 15–19	Ps. *28*; 30 *alt.* Ps. 139 Deut. ch. 33 1 John 4. 7–end
	W			[Ezek. 36. 22–28 Matt. 12. 22–32]
11	Sa	**BARNABAS THE APOSTLE**	Job 29. 11–16 *or* Acts 11. 19–end Ps. 112 Acts 11. 19–end *or* Gal. 2. 1–10 John 15. 12–17	*MP*: Ps. 100; 101; 117 Jer. 9. 23–24 Acts 4. 32–end
	R			
12	S	**DAY OF PENTECOST** *The reading from Acts must be* *used as either the first or second* *reading at the Principal Service.*	Acts 2. 1–21 *or* Num. 11. 24–30 Ps. 104. 26–34, 36, 37b (*or* 104. 26–end) 1 Cor. 12. 3b–13 *or* Acts 2. 1–21 John 20. 19–23 *or* John 7. 37–39	*MP*: Ps. 87 Gen. 11. 1–9 Acts 10. 34–end
	R			
13 DEL 11	M		2 Cor. 6. 1–10 Ps. 98 Matt. 5. 38–42	Ps. 123; 124; 125; *126* 2 Chron. 17. 1–12 Rom. 1. 1–17
	G			
14	Tu	*Richard Baxter, Puritan Divine, 1691*	2 Cor. 8. 1–9 Ps. 146 Matt. 5. 43–end	Ps. *132*; 133 2 Chron. 18. 1–27 Rom. 1. 18–end
	G			
15	W	*Evelyn Underhill, Spiritual Writer, 1941*	2 Cor. 9. 6–11 Ps. 112 Matt. 6. 1–6, 16–18	Ps. 119. 153–end 2 Chron. 18.28 – 19.end Rom. 2. 1–16
	G			

Second Service Evening Prayer		Calendar and Holy Communion	Morning Prayer	Evening Prayer
Ps. 18 *alt.* Ps. **105**† *(or* 103*)* Num. 22. 1–35 Luke 7. 36–end	W		Deut. 31. 1–13 1 John 2. 18–end [Num. 27. 15–end 1 Cor. ch. 3]	Num. 22. 1–35 Luke 7. 36–end
Ps. 68 *alt.* Ps. 107† Num. 22.36 – 23.12 Luke 8. 1–15	W		Deut. 31. 14–29 1 John 3. 1–10 [1 Sam. 10. 1–10 1 Cor. 12. 1–13]	Num. 22.36 – 23.12 Luke 8. 1–15
Ps. 36; **46** *alt.* Ps. 119. 129–152 Num. 23. 13–end Luke 8. 16–25	W		Deut. 31.30 – 32.14 1 John 3. 11–end [1 Kings 19. 1–18 Matt. 3. 13–end]	Num. 23. 13–end Luke 8. 16–25
Ps. 139 *alt.* Ps. 114; **116**; 117 Num. ch. 24 Luke 8. 26–39	W		Deut. 32. 15–47 1 John 4. 1–6 [Ezek. 11. 14–20 Matt. 9.35 – 10.20]	Num. ch. 24 Luke 8. 26–39
Ps. 147 *alt.* Ps. **130**; 131; 137 Num. 27. 12–end Luke 8. 40–end *or First EP of Barnabas*: Ps. 1; 15 Isa. 42. 5–12 Acts 14. 8–end **R ct**	W		Deut. ch. 33 1 John 4. 7–end [Ezek. 36. 22–28 Matt. 12. 22–32]	Num. 27. 12–end Luke 8. 40–end *or First EP of Barnabas*: (Ps. 1; 15) Isa. 42. 5–12 Acts 14. 8–end **R ct**
First EP of Pentecost Ps. 48 Deut. 16. 9–15 John 15.26 – 16.15 **R ct**	R	**BARNABAS THE APOSTLE** Job 29. 11–16 Ps. 112 Acts 11. 22–end John 15. 12–16	(Ps. 100; 101; 117) Jer. 9. 23–24 Acts 4. 32–end	*First EP of Pentecost* Ps. 48 Deut. 16. 9–15 John 15.26 – 16.15 **R ct**
EP: Ps. 67; 133 Joel 2. 21–end Acts 2. 14–21 [22–38] *Gospel*: Luke 24. 44–end	R	**WHIT SUNDAY** Deut. 16. 9–12 Ps. 122 Acts 2. 1–11 John 14. 15–31a	Ps. 87 Gen. 11. 1–9 Acts 10. 34–end	Ps. 67; 133 Num. 11. 24–30 Acts 2. 14–21 [22–38]
Ps. **127**; 128; 129 Josh. ch. 1 Luke 9. 18–27	R	**Monday in Whitsun Week** Acts 10. 34–end John 3. 16–21	Ezek. 11. 14–20 Acts 2. 12–36	Exod. 35.30 – 36.1 Acts 2. 37–end
Ps. (134); **135** Josh. ch. 2 Luke 9. 28–36	R	**Tuesday in Whitsun Week** Acts 8. 14–17 John 10. 1–10	Ezek. 37. 1–14 1 Cor. 12. 1–13	2 Sam. 23. 1–5 1 Cor. 12.27 – 13.end
Ps. 136 Josh. ch. 3 Luke 9. 37–50	R	Ember Day Ember CEG *or* Acts 2. 14–21 John 6. 44–51	2 Chron. 18.28 – 19.end Rom. 2. 1–16	Josh. ch. 3 Luke 9. 37–50

June 2011

				Sunday Principal Service Weekday Eucharist	Third Service Morning Prayer

16 Th **Richard, Bishop of Chichester, 1253**
Joseph Butler, Bishop of Durham, Philosopher, 1752
Com. Bishop   *or*   2 Cor. 11. 1–11   Ps. *143*; 146
also John 21. 15–19   Ps. 111   2 Chron. 20. 1–23
Gw   Matt. 6. 7–15   Rom. 2. 17–end

---

17 F *Samuel and Henrietta Barnett, Social Reformers, 1913 and 1936*

2 Cor. 11. 18, 21b–30   Ps. *142*; 144
Ps. 34. 1–6   2 Chron. 22.10 – 23.end
Matt. 6. 19–23   Rom. 3. 1–20

G

---

18 Sa *Bernard Mizeki, Apostle of the MaShona, Martyr, 1896*
2 Cor. 12. 1–10   Ps. 147
Ps. 89. 20–33   2 Chron. 24. 1–22
Matt. 6. 24–end   Rom. 3. 21–end

G

---

19 S **TRINITY SUNDAY**
Isa. 40. 12–17, 27–end   *MP*: Ps. 86. 8–13
Ps. 8   Exod. 3. 1–6, 13–15
2 Cor. 13. 11–end   John 17. 1–11
ꟿ   Matt. 28. 16–20

---

20 M
DEL 12   Gen. 12. 1–9   Ps. *1*; 2; 3
G   Ps. 33. 12–end   2 Chron. 26. 1–21
                           Matt. 7. 1–5   Rom. 4. 1–12

---

21 Tu
                           Gen. 13. 2, 5–end   Ps. *5*; 6; (8)
G   Ps. 15   2 Chron. ch. 28
                           Matt. 7. 6, 12–14   Rom. 4. 13–end

---

22 W **Alban, first Martyr of Britain, c. 250**
Ember Day*
Com. Martyr   *or*   Gen. 15. 1–12, 17–18   Ps. 119. 1–32
esp. 2 Tim. 2. 3–13   Ps. 105. 1–9   2 Chron. 29. 1–19
John 12. 24–26   Matt. 7. 15–20   Rom. 5. 1–11

Gr *or* R

---

23 Th DAY OF THANKSGIVING FOR HOLY COMMUNION (CORPUS CHRISTI)
Etheldreda, Abbess of Ely, c. 678
Gen. 14. 18–20   *MP*: Ps. 147
Ps. 116. 10–end   Deut. 8. 2–16
1 Cor. 11. 23–26   1 Cor. 10. 1–17
John 6. 51–58

W

or Com. Religious   *or*   Gen. 16. 1–12, 15–16   Ps. 14; *15*; 16
also Matt. 25. 1–13   Ps. 106. 1–5   2 Chron. 29. 20–end
                                   Matt. 7. 21–end   Rom. 5. 12–end

Gw

---

*For Ember Day provision, see p. 13.

Second Service Evening Prayer		Calendar and Holy Communion	Morning Prayer	Evening Prayer
Ps. *138*; 140; 141 Josh. 4.1 – 5.1 Luke 9. 51–end	R	Acts 2. 22–28 Luke 9. 1–6	2 Chron. 20. 1–23 Rom. 2. 17–end	Josh. 4.1 – 5.1 Luke 9. 51–end
Ps. 145 Josh. 5. 2–end Luke 10. 1–16	R	**Alban, first Martyr of Britain, c. 250** Ember Day Com. Martyr *or* Ember CEG *or* Acts 8. 5–8 Luke 5. 17–26	2 Chron. 22.10 – 23.end Rom. 3. 1–20	Josh. 5. 2–end Luke 10. 1–16
First EP of Trinity Sunday Ps. 97; 98 Exod. 34. 1–10 Mark 1. 1–13 ℣ ct	R	Ember Day Ember CEG *or* Acts 13. 44–end Matt. 20. 29–end	2 Chron. 24. 1–22 Rom. 3. 21–end	*First EP of Trinity Sunday* Ps. 97; 98 Exod. 34. 1–10 Mark 1. 1–13 ℣ ct
EP: Ps. 93; 150 Isa. 6. 1–8 John 16. 5–15	℣	**TRINITY SUNDAY** Isa. 6. 1–8 Ps. 8 Rev. 4. 1–11 John 3. 1–15	Ps. 86. 8–13 Exod. 3. 1–6, 13–15 John 17. 1–11	Ps. 93; 150 Isa. 40. 12–17, 27–end John 16. 5–15
Ps. *4*; 7 Josh. 7. 1–15 Luke 10. 25–37	Gr	**Translation of Edward, King of the West Saxons, 979** Com. Martyr	2 Chron. 26. 1–21 Rom. 4. 1–12	Josh. 7. 1–15 Luke 10. 25–37
Ps. *9*; 10† Josh. 7. 16–end Luke 10. 38–end	G		2 Chron. ch. 28 Rom. 4. 13–end	Josh. 7. 16–end Luke 10. 38–end
Ps. *11*; 12; 13 Josh. 8. 1–29 Luke 11. 1–13 *or First EP of Corpus Christi* Ps. 110; 111 Exod. 16. 2–15 John 6. 22–35 W ct	G		2 Chron. 29. 1–19 Rom. 5. 1–11	Josh. 8. 1–29 Luke 11. 1–13
		To celebrate Corpus Christi, see *Common Worship* provision.		
EP: Ps. 23; 42; 43 Prov. 9. 1–5 Luke 9. 11–17 *or First EP of The Birth of John the Baptist* Ps. 71 Judges 13. 2–7, 24–end Luke 1. 5–25 ct Ps. 18† Josh. 8. 30–end Luke 11. 14–28 *or First EP of The Birth of John the Baptist* Ps. 71 Judges 13. 2–7, 24–end Luke 1. 5–25 W ct	G		2 Chron. 29. 20–end Rom. 5. 12–end	Josh. 8. 30–end Luke 11. 14–28 *or First EP of The Birth of John the Baptist* (Ps. 71) Judges 13. 2–7, 24–end Luke 1. 5–25 W ct

June 2011

			Sunday Principal Service Weekday Eucharist	Third Service Morning Prayer

24 F **THE BIRTH OF JOHN THE BAPTIST**
Ember Day*

Isa. 40. 1–11
Ps. 85. 7–end
Acts 13. 14b–26
or Gal. 3. 23–end
W   Luke 1. 57–66, 80

MP: Ps. 50; 149
Ecclus. 48. 1–10
or Mal. 3. 1–6
Luke 3. 1–17

---

25 Sa Ember Day*

Gen. 18. 1–15
Canticle: Luke 1. 46b–55
Matt. 8. 5–17

G or R

Ps. 20; 21; **23**
2 Chron. 32. 1–22
Rom. 6. 15–end

---

26 S **THE FIRST SUNDAY AFTER TRINITY (Proper 8)**

Track 1
Gen. 22. 1–14
Ps. 13
Rom. 6. 12–end
Matt. 10. 40–end
G

Track 2
Jer. 28. 5–9
Ps. 89. 1–4, 15–18
(or 89. 8–18)
Rom. 6. 12–end
Matt. 10. 40–end

Ps. 52; 53
Deut. 15. 1–11
Acts 27. [13–32] 33–end

---

27 M *Cyril, Bishop of Alexandria, Teacher, 444*
DEL 13   G

Gen. 18. 16–end
Ps. 103. 6–17
Matt. 8. 18–22

Ps. 27; **30**
2 Chron. 33. 1–13
Rom. 7. 1–6

---

28 Tu **Irenaeus, Bishop of Lyons, Teacher, c. 200**
Com. Teacher   or
also 2 Pet. 1. 16–21

Gen. 19. 15–29
Ps. 26
Matt. 8. 23–27

Ps. 32; **36**
2 Chron. 34. 1–18
Rom. 7. 7–end

Gw

---

29 W **PETER AND PAUL, APOSTLES**

Zech. 4. 1–6a, 10b–end
or Acts 12. 1–11
Ps. 125
Acts 12. 1–11
or 2 Tim. 4. 6–8, 17–18
R   Matt. 16. 13–19

MP: Ps. 71; 113
Isa. 49. 1–6
Acts 11. 1–18

or, if Peter is commemorated alone:

Ezek. 3. 22–end
or Acts 12. 1–11
Ps. 125
Acts 12. 1–11
or 1 Pet. 2. 19–end
R   Matt. 16. 13–19

MP: Ps. 71; 113
Isa. 49. 1–6
Acts 11. 1–18

---

30 Th

Gen. 22. 1–19
Ps. 116. 1–7
G   Matt. 9. 1–8

Ps. 37†
2 Chron. 35. 1–19
Rom. 8. 12–17

July 2011

1 F *Henry, John and Henry Venn the Younger, Priests, Evangelical Divines, 1797, 1813 and 1873*

Gen. 23. 1–4, 19; 24. 1–8,
62–end
Ps. 106. 1–5
G   Matt. 9. 9–13

Ps. 31
2 Chron. 35.20 – 36.10
Rom. 8. 18–30

---

*For Ember Day provision, see p. 13.

Second Service Evening Prayer		Calendar and Holy Communion	Morning Prayer	Evening Prayer
		THE BIRTH OF JOHN THE BAPTIST		
EP: Ps. 80; 82 Mal. ch. 4 Matt. 11. 2–19	W	Isa. 40. 1–11 Ps. 80. 1–7 Acts 13. 22–26 Luke 1. 57–80	(Ps. 50; 149) Ecclus. 48. 1–10 or Mal. 3. 1–6 Luke 3. 1–17	(Ps. 82) Mal. ch. 4 Matt. 11. 2–19
Ps. 24; 25 Josh. 10. 1–15 Luke 11. 37–end ct	G		2 Chron. 32. 1–22 Rom. 6. 15–end	Josh. 10. 1–15 Luke 11. 37–end ct
Ps. 50 (or 50. 1–15) 1 Sam. 28. 3–19 Luke 17. 20–end	G	THE FIRST SUNDAY AFTER TRINITY 2 Sam. 9. 6–end Ps. 41. 1–4 1 John 4. 7–end Luke 16. 19–31	Ps. 52; 53 Deut. 15. 1–11 Acts 27. [13–32] 33–end	Ps. 50 (or 50. 1–15) 1 Sam. 28. 3–19 Luke 17. 20–end
Ps. 26; 28; 29 Josh. ch. 14 Luke 12. 1–12	G		2 Chron. 33. 1–13 Rom. 7. 1–6	Josh. ch. 14 Luke 12. 1–12
Ps. 33 Josh. 21.43 – 22.8 Luke 12. 13–21 or First EP of Peter and Paul Ps. 66; 67 Ezek. 3. 4–11 Gal. 1.13 – 2.8 or, for Peter alone: Acts 9. 32–end R ct	G		2 Chron. 34. 1–18 Rom. 7. 7–end	Josh. 21.43 – 22.8 Luke 12. 13–21 or First EP of Peter (Ps. 66; 67) Ezek. 3. 4–11 Acts 9. 32–end R ct
EP: Ps. 124; 138 Ezek. 34. 11–16 John 21. 15–22 EP: Ps. 124; 138 Ezek. 34. 11–16 John 21. 15–22	R	PETER THE APOSTLE Ezek. 3. 4–11 Ps. 125 Acts 12. 1–11 Matt. 16. 13–19	(Ps. 71; 113) Isa. 49. 1–6 Acts 11. 1–18	(Ps. 124; 138) Ezek. 34. 11–16 John 21. 15–22
Ps. 39; 40 Josh. ch. 23 Luke 12. 32–40	G		2 Chron. 35. 1–19 Rom. 8. 12–17	Josh. ch. 23 Luke 12. 32–40
Ps. 35 Josh. 24. 1–28 Luke 12. 41–48	G		2 Chron. 35.20 – 36.10 Rom. 8. 18–30	Josh. 24. 1–28 Luke 12. 41–48

July 2011

			Sunday Principal Service Weekday Eucharist	Third Service Morning Prayer
2	Sa		Gen. 27. 1–5a, 15–29 Ps. 135. 1–6 Matt. 9. 14–17	Ps. 41; **42**; 43 2 Chron. 36. 11–end Rom. 8. 31–end
	G			
3	S	THOMAS THE APOSTLE**	Hab. 2. 1–4 Ps. 31. 1–6 Eph. 2. 19–end John 20. 24–29	MP: Ps. 92; 146 2 Sam. 15. 17–21 or Ecclus. ch. 2 John 11. 1–16
	R	or, for The Second Sunday after Trinity (Proper 9):		
		Track 1 Gen. 24. 34–38, 42–49, 58–end Ps. 45. 10–17 or Canticle: Song of Sol. 2. 8–13 Rom. 7. 15–25a	Track 2 Zech. 9. 9–12 Ps. 145. 8–15 Rom. 7. 15–25a Matt. 11. 16–19, 25–end	Ps. 55. 1–15, 18–22 Deut. 24. 10–end Acts 28. 1–16
	G	Matt. 11. 16–19, 25–end		
4 DEL 14	M		Gen. 28. 10–end Ps. 91. 1–10	Ps. 44 Ezra ch. 1
	G		Matt. 9. 18–26	Rom. 9. 1–18
5	Tu		Gen. 32. 22–end Ps. 17. 1–8	Ps. **48**; 52 Ezra ch. 3
	G		Matt. 9. 32–end	Rom. 9. 19–end
6	W	Thomas More, Scholar, and John Fisher, Bishop of Rochester, Reformation Martyrs, 1535	Gen. 41. 55–end; 42. 5–7, 17–end Ps. 33. 1–4, 18–end	Ps. 119. 57–80 Ezra 4. 1–5 Rom. 10. 1–10
	G		Matt. 10. 1–7	
7	Th	***	Gen. 44. 18–21, 23–29; 45. 1–5 Ps. 105. 11–17	Ps. 56; **57**; (63†) Ezra 4. 7–end
	G		Matt. 10. 7–15	Rom. 10. 11–end
8	F		Gen. 46. 1–7, 28–30 Ps. 37. 3–6, 27–28	Ps. **51**; 54 Ezra ch. 5
	G		Matt. 10. 16–23	Rom. 11. 1–12
9	Sa		Gen. 49. 29–end; 50. 15–25 Ps. 105. 1–7	Ps. 68 Ezra ch. 6
	G		Matt. 10. 24–33	Rom. 11. 13–24
10	S	THE THIRD SUNDAY AFTER TRINITY (Proper 10) Track 1 Gen. 25. 19–end Ps. 119. 105–112 Rom. 8. 1–11	Track 2 Isa. 55. 10–13 Ps. 65 (or 65. 8–end) Rom. 8. 1–11	Ps. 64; 65 Deut. 28. 1–14 Acts 28. 17–end
	G	Matt. 13. 1–9, 18–23	Matt. 13. 1–9, 18–23	
11 DEL 15	M	**Benedict of Nursia, Abbot of Monte Cassino, Father of Western Monasticism, c. 550** Com. Religious also 1 Cor. 3. 10–11	or Exod. 1. 8–14, 22 Ps. 124	Ps. 71 Ezra ch. 7
	Gw	Luke 18. 18–22	Matt. 10.34 – 11.1	Rom. 11. 25–end
12	Tu		Exod. 2. 1–15 Ps. 69. 1–2, 31–end	Ps. 73 Ezra 8. 15–end
	G		Matt. 11. 20–24	Rom. 12. 1–8

*Common Worship Morning and Evening Prayer provision for 31 May may be used.
**Thomas the Apostle may be celebrated on 21 December instead of 3 July.
***Thomas Becket may be celebrated on 7 July instead of 29 December.

Second Service Evening Prayer	Calendar and Holy Communion	Morning Prayer	Evening Prayer
	The Visitation of the Blessed Virgin Mary*		
Ps. 45; **46**	1 Sam. 2. 1–3	2 Chron. 36. 11–end	Josh. 24. 29–end
Josh. 24. 29–end	Ps. 113	Rom. 8. 31–end	Luke 12. 49–end
Luke 12. 49–end	Gal. 4. 1–5		
ct	Luke 1. 39–45		
or First EP of Thomas			
Ps. 27			
Isa. ch. 35			
Heb. 10.35 – 11.1			
R ct	**Gw**		**ct**
	THE SECOND SUNDAY AFTER TRINITY		
EP: Ps. 139	Gen. 12. 1–4	Ps. 55. 1–15, 18–22	Ps. 56; [57]
Job 42. 1–6	Ps. 120	Deut. 24. 10–end	2 Sam. 2. 1–11; 3. 1
1 Pet. 1. 3–12	1 John 3. 13–end	Acts 28. 1–16	Luke 18.31 – 19.10
	Luke 14. 16–24		
Ps. 56; [57]			
2 Sam. 2. 1–11; 3. 1			
Luke 18.31 – 19.10			
	G		
	Translation of Martin, Bishop of Tours, c. 397		
Ps. **47**; 49	Com. Bishop	Ezra ch. 1	Judg. ch. 2
Judg. ch. 2		Rom. 9. 1–18	Luke 13. 1–9
Luke 13. 1–9	**Gw**		
Ps. 50		Ezra ch. 3	Judg. 4. 1–23
Judg. 4. 1–23		Rom. 9. 19–end	Luke 13. 10–21
Luke 13. 10–21	**G**		
Ps. **59**; 60; (67)		Ezra 4. 1–5	Judg. ch. 5
Judg. ch. 5		Rom. 10. 1–10	Luke 13. 22–end
Luke 13. 22–end	**G**		
Ps. 61; **62**; 64		Ezra 4. 7–end	Judg. 6. 1–24
Judg. 6. 1–24		Rom. 10. 11–end	Luke 14. 1–11
Luke 14. 1–11	**G**		
Ps. 38		Ezra ch. 5	Judg. 6. 25–end
Judg. 6. 25–end		Rom. 11. 1–12	Luke 14. 12–24
Luke 14. 12–24	**G**		
Ps. 65; **66**		Ezra ch. 6	Judg. ch. 7
Judg. ch. 7		Rom. 11. 13–24	Luke 14. 25–end
Luke 14. 25–end			
ct	**G**		ct
	THE THIRD SUNDAY AFTER TRINITY		
Ps. 60; [63]	2 Chron. 33. 9–13	Ps. 64; 65	Ps. 60; [63]
2 Sam. 7. 18–end	Ps. 55. 17–23	Deut. 28. 1–14	2 Sam. 7. 18–end
Luke 19.41 – 20.8	1 Pet. 5. 5b–11	Acts 28. 17–end	Luke 20. 1–8
	Luke 15. 1–10		
	G		
Ps. **72**; 75		Ezra ch. 7	Judg. 8. 22–end
Judg. 8. 22–end		Rom. 11. 25–end	Luke 15. 1–10
Luke 15. 1–10	**G**		
Ps. 74		Ezra 8. 15–end	Judg. 9. 1–21
Judg. 9. 1–21		Rom. 12. 1–8	Luke 15. 11–end
Luke 15. 11–end	**G**		

July 2011

		Sunday Principal Service / Weekday Eucharist	Third Service / Morning Prayer
13	W	Exod. 3. 1–6, 9–12	Ps. 77
		Ps. 103. 1–7	Ezra ch. 9
	G	Matt. 11. 25–27	Rom. 12. 9–end

14 Th — **John Keble, Priest, Tractarian, Poet, 1866**

		Com. Pastor *or*	Exod. 3. 13–20	Ps. 78. 1–39†
		also Lam. 3. 19–26	Ps. 105. 1–2, 23	Ezra 10. 1–7
	Gw	Matt. 5. 1–8	Matt. 11. 28–end	Rom. 13. 1–7

15 F — **Swithun, Bishop of Winchester, c. 862**
Bonaventure, Friar, Bishop, Teacher, 1274

		Com. Bishop *or*	Exod. 11.10 – 12.14	Ps. 55
		also James 5. 7–11, 13–18	Ps. 116. 10–end	Neh. ch. 1
	Gw		Matt. 12. 1–8	Rom. 13. 8–end

16 Sa — *Osmund, Bishop of Salisbury, 1099*

		Exod. 12. 37–42	Ps. *76*; 79
		Ps. 136. 1–4, 10–15	Neh. ch. 2
	G	Matt. 12. 14–21	Rom. 14. 1–12

17 S — THE FOURTH SUNDAY AFTER TRINITY (**Proper 11**)

	Track 1	Track 2	
	Gen. 28. 10–19a	Wisd. 12. 13, 16–19	Ps. 71
	Ps. 139. 1–11, 23–24 (or 139. 1–11)	*or* Isa. 44. 6–8	Deut. 30. 1–10
	Rom. 8. 12–25	Ps. 86. 11–17	1 Pet. 3. 8–18
	Matt. 13. 24–30, 36–43	Rom. 8. 12–25	
G		Matt. 13. 24–30, 36–43	

18 M — *Elizabeth Ferard, first Deaconess of the Church of England, Founder of the Community of St Andrew, 1883*
DEL 16

		Exod. 14. 5–18	Ps. *80*; 82
		Ps. 136. 1–4, 10–15	Neh. ch. 4
		or Canticle: Exod. 15. 1–6	Rom. 14. 13–end
	G	Matt. 12. 38–42	

19 Tu — **Gregory, Bishop of Nyssa, and his sister Macrina, Deaconess, Teachers, c. 394 and c. 379**

		Com. Teacher *or*	Exod. 14.21 – 15.1	Ps. 87; *89. 1–18*
		esp. 1 Cor. 2. 9–13	Ps. 105. 37–44	Neh. ch. 5
		also Wisd. 9. 3–17	*or* Canticle:	Rom. 15. 1–13
			Exod. 15. 8–10, 12, 17	
	Gw		Matt. 12. 46–end	

20 W — *Margaret of Antioch, Martyr, 4th century; Bartolomé de las Casas, Apostle to the Indies, 1566*

		Exod. 16. 1–5, 9–15	Ps. 119. 105–128
		Ps. 78. 17–31	Neh. 6.1 – 7.4
	G	Matt. 13. 1–9	Rom. 15. 14–21

21 Th

		Exod. 19. 1–2, 9–11, 16–20	Ps. 90; *92*
		Canticle: Bless the Lord	Neh. 7.73b – 8.end
		Matt. 13. 10–17	Rom. 15. 22–end
	G		

22 F — MARY MAGDALENE

		Song of Sol. 3. 1–4	*MP*: Ps. 30; 32; 150
		Ps. 42. 1–10	1 Sam. 16. 14–end
		2 Cor. 5. 14–17	Luke 8. 1–3
	W	John 20. 1–2, 11–18	

23 Sa — *Bridget of Sweden, Abbess of Vadstena, 1373*

		Exod. 24. 3–8	Ps. 96; *97*; 100
		Ps. 50. 1–6, 14–15	Neh. 9. 24–end
	G	Matt. 13. 24–30	Rom. 16. 17–end

Second Service Evening Prayer	Calendar and Holy Communion	Morning Prayer	Evening Prayer
Ps. 119. 81–104 Judg. 9. 22–end Luke 16. 1–18	G	Ezra ch. 9 Rom. 12. 9–end	Judg. 9. 22–end Luke 16. 1–18
Ps. 78. 40–end† Judg. 11. 1–11 Luke 16. 19–end	G	Ezra 10. 1–7 Rom. 13. 1–7	Judg. 11. 1–11 Luke 16. 19–end
Ps. 69 Judg. 11. 29–end Luke 17. 1–10	**Swithun, Bishop of Winchester, c. 862** Com. Bishop Gw	Neh. ch. 1 Rom. 13. 8–end	Judg. 11. 29–end Luke 17. 1–10
Ps. 81; *84* Judg. 12. 1–7 Luke 17. 11–19 ct	G	Neh. ch. 2 Rom. 14. 1–12	Judg. 12. 1–7 Luke 17. 11–19 ct
Ps. 67; [70] 1 Kings 2. 10–12; 3. 16–end Acts 4. 1–22 *Gospel:* Mark 6. 30–34, 53–end	THE FOURTH SUNDAY AFTER TRINITY Gen. 3. 17–19 Ps. 79. 8–10 Rom. 8. 18–23 Luke 6. 36–42 G	Ps. 71 Deut. 30. 1–10 1 Pet. 3. 13–22	Ps. 67; [70] 1 Kings 2. 10–12; 3. 16–end Acts 4. 1–22
Ps. *85*; 86 Judg. 13. 1–24 Luke 17. 20–end	G	Neh. ch. 4 Rom. 14. 13–end	Judg. 13. 1–24 Luke 17. 20–end
Ps. 89. 19–end Judg. ch. 14 Luke 18. 1–14	G	Neh. ch. 5 Rom. 15. 1–13	Judg. ch. 14 Luke 18. 1–14
Ps. *91*; 93 Judg. 15.1 – 16.3 Luke 18. 15–30	**Margaret of Antioch, Martyr, 4th century** Com. Virgin Martyr Gr	Neh. 6.1 – 7.4 Rom. 15. 14–21	Judg. 15.1 – 16.3 Luke 18. 15–30
Ps. 94 Judg. 16. 4–end Luke 18. 31–end *or First EP of Mary* *Magdalene* Ps. 139 Isa. 25. 1–9 2 Cor. 1. 3–7 **W** ct	G	Neh. 7.73b – 8.end Rom. 15. 22–end	Judg. 16. 4–end Luke 18. 31–end *or First EP of Mary* *Magdalene* (Ps. 139) Isa. 25. 1–9 2 Cor. 1. 3–7 **W** ct
EP: Ps. 63 Zeph. 3. 14–end Mark 15.40 – 16.7	MARY MAGDALENE Zeph. 3. 14–end Ps. 30. 1–5 2 Cor. 5. 14–17 W John 20. 11–18	(Ps. 30; 32; 150) 1 Sam. 16. 14–end Luke 8. 1–3	(Ps. 63) Song of Sol. 3. 1–4 Mark 15.40 – 16.7
Ps. 104 Judg. 18. 1–20, 27–end Luke 19. 11–27 ct	G	Neh. 9. 24–end Rom. 16. 17–end	Judg. 18. 1–20, 27–end Luke 19. 11–27 ct

July 2011

			Sunday Principal Service Weekday Eucharist	Third Service Morning Prayer

24 S — THE FIFTH SUNDAY AFTER TRINITY (Proper 12)

Track 1	Track 2	
Gen. 29. 15–28	1 Kings 3. 5–12	Ps. 77
Ps. 105. 1–11, 45b (or 105. 1–11)	Ps. 119. 129–136	Song of Sol. ch. 2
or Ps. 128	Rom. 8. 26–end	or 1 Macc. 2. [1–14] 15–22
Rom. 8. 26–end	Matt. 13. 31–33, 44–52	1 Pet. 4. 7–14
Matt. 13. 31–33, 44–52		

G

25 M — JAMES THE APOSTLE

DEL 17

	Jer. 45. 1–5	MP: Ps. 7; 29; 117
	or Acts 11.27 – 12.2	2 Kings 1. 9–15
	Ps. 126	Luke 9. 46–56
	Acts 11.27 – 12.2	
	or 2 Cor. 4. 7–15	
R | Matt. 20. 20–28 | |

26 Tu — **Anne and Joachim, Parents of the Blessed Virgin Mary**

Zeph. 3. 14–18a	or	Exod. 33. 7–11; 34. 5–9, 28	Ps. 106† (or 103)
Ps. 127		Ps. 103. 8–12	Neh. 13. 1–14
Rom. 8. 28–30		Matt. 13. 36–43	2 Cor. 1.15 – 2.4
Gw Matt. 13. 16–17			

27 W — *Brooke Foss Westcott, Bishop of Durham, Teacher, 1901*

	Exod. 34. 29–end	Ps. 110; 111; 112
	Ps. 99	Neh. 13. 15–end
G	Matt. 13. 44–46	2 Cor. 2. 5–end

28 Th

	Exod. 40. 16–21, 34–end	Ps. 113; 115
	Ps. 84. 1–6	Esther ch. 1
G	Matt. 13. 47–53	2 Cor. ch. 3

29 F — **Mary, Martha and Lazarus, Companions of Our Lord**

Isa. 25. 6–9	or	Lev. 23. 1, 4–11, 15–16,	Ps. 139
Ps. 49. 1–10, 16		27, 34–37	Esther ch. 2
Heb. 2. 10–15		Ps. 81. 1–8	2 Cor. ch. 4
Gw John 12. 1–8		Matt. 13. 54–end	

30 Sa — **William Wilberforce, Social Reformer, 1833**

Com. Saint	or	Lev. 25. 1, 8–17	Ps. 120; 121; 122
also Job 31. 16–23		Ps. 67	Esther ch. 3
Gal. 3. 26–end; 4. 6–7		Matt. 14. 1–12	2 Cor. ch. 5
Gw Luke 4. 16–21			

31 S — THE SIXTH SUNDAY AFTER TRINITY (Proper 13)

Track 1	Track 2	
Gen. 32. 22–31	Isa. 55. 1–5	Ps. 85
Ps. 17. 1–7, 16 (or 17. 1–7)	Ps. 145. 8–9, 15–end	Song of Sol. 5. 2–end
Rom. 9. 1–5	(or 145. 15–end)	or 1 Macc. 3. 1–12
Matt. 14. 13–21	Rom. 9. 1–5	2 Pet. 1. 1–15
G	Matt. 14. 13–21	

August 2011

1 M

DEL 18

	Num. 11. 4–15	Ps. 123; 124; 125; 126
	Ps. 81. 11–end	Esther ch. 4
	Matt. 14. 13–21	2 Cor. 6.1 – 7.1
G	(or 14. 22–end)	

2 Tu

	Num. 12. 1–13	Ps. 132; 133
	Ps. 51. 1–8	Esther ch. 5
	Matt. 14. 22–end	2 Cor. 7. 2–end
G	or 15. 1–2, 10–14	

3 W

	Num. 13.1–2, 10–14,	Ps. 119. 153–end
	25 – 14.1, 26–35	Esther 6. 1–13
	Ps. 106. 14–24	2 Cor. 8. 1–15
G	Matt. 15. 21–28	

Second Service Evening Prayer	Calendar and Holy Communion	Morning Prayer	Evening Prayer
	THE FIFTH SUNDAY AFTER TRINITY		
Ps. 75; [76]	1 Kings 19. 19–21	Ps. 77	Ps. 75; [76]
1 Kings 6. 11–14, 23–end	Ps. 84. 8–end	Song of Sol. ch. 2	1 Kings 6. 11–14,
Acts 12. 1–17	1 Pet. 3. 8–15a	or 1 Macc. 2. [1–14]	23–end
Gospel: John 6. 1–21	Luke 5. 1–11	15–22	Acts 12. 1–17
or First EP of James		1 Pet. 4. 7–14	or First EP of James
Ps. 144			Ps. 144
Deut. 30. 11–end			Deut. 30. 11–end
Mark 5. 21–end			Mark 5. 21–end
R ct	G		**R ct**
	JAMES THE APOSTLE		
EP: Ps. 94	2 Kings 1. 9–15	(Ps. 7; 29; 117)	(Ps. 94)
Jer. 26. 1–15	Ps. 15	Jer. 45. 1–5	Jer. 26. 1–15
Mark 1. 14–20	Acts 11.27 – 12.3a	Luke 9. 46–56	Mark 1. 14–20
	Matt. 20. 20–28		
	R		
	Anne, Mother of the Blessed Virgin Mary		
Ps. 107†	Com. Saint	Neh. 13. 1–14	1 Sam. 1.21 – 2.11
1 Sam. 1.21 – 2.11		2 Cor. 1.15 – 2.4	Luke 19. 41–end
Luke 19. 41–end			
	Gw		
Ps. 119. 129–152		Neh. 13. 15–end	1 Sam. 2. 12–26
1 Sam. 2. 12–26		2 Cor. 2. 5–end	Luke 20. 1–8
Luke 20. 1–8	G		
Ps. 114; *116*; 117		Esther ch. 1	1 Sam. 2. 27–end
1 Sam. 2. 27–end		2 Cor. ch. 3	Luke 20. 9–19
Luke 20. 9–19	G		
Ps. *130*; 131; 137		Esther ch. 2	1 Sam. 3.1 – 4.1a
1 Sam. 3.1 – 4.1a		2 Cor. ch. 4	Luke 20. 20–26
Luke 20. 20–26			
	G		
Ps. 118		Esther ch. 3	1 Sam. 4. 1b–end
1 Sam. 4. 1b–end		2 Cor. ch. 5	Luke 20. 27–40
Luke 20. 27–40			
ct	G		ct
	THE SIXTH SUNDAY AFTER TRINITY		
Ps. 80	Gen. 4. 2b–15	Ps. 85	Ps. 80
(or 80. 1–8)	Ps. 90. 12–end	Song of Sol. 5. 2–end	(or 80. 1–8)
1 Kings 10. 1–13	Rom. 6. 3–11	or 1 Macc. 3. 1–12	1 Kings 10. 1–13
Acts 13. 1–13	Matt. 5. 20–26	2 Pet. 1. 1–15	Acts 13. 1–13
Gospel: John 6. 24–35	G		
Ps. *127*; 128; 129	Lammas Day	Esther ch. 4	1 Sam. ch. 5
1 Sam. ch. 5		2 Cor. 6.1 – 7.1	Luke 20.41 – 21.4
Luke 20.41 – 21.4			
	G		
Ps. (134); *135*		Esther ch. 5	1 Sam. 6. 1–16
1 Sam. 6. 1–16		2 Cor. 7. 2–end	Luke 21. 5–19
Luke 21. 5–19	G		
Ps. 136		Esther 6. 1–13	1 Sam. ch. 7
1 Sam. ch. 7		2 Cor. 8. 1–15	Luke 21. 20–28
Luke 21. 20–28	G		

August 2011

			Sunday Principal Service / Weekday Eucharist	Third Service / Morning Prayer

4 Th — *John-Baptiste Vianney, Curé d'Ars, Spiritual Guide, 1859*
Num. 20. 1–13
Ps. 95. 1, 8–end
G Matt. 16. 13–23
Ps. *143*; 146
Esther 6.14 – 7.end
2 Cor. 8.16 – 9.5

5 F — **Oswald, King of Northumbria, Martyr, 642**
Com. Martyr   *or*   Deut. 4. 32–40
esp. I Pet. 4. 12–end   Ps. 77. 11–end
Matt. 16. 24–end
Ps. 142; *144*
Esther ch. 8
2 Cor. 9. 6–end

Gr

6 Sa — THE TRANSFIGURATION OF OUR LORD
Dan. 7. 9–10, 13–14
Ps. 97
2 Pet. 1. 16–19
Luke 9. 28–36
𝖜
MP: Ps. 27; 150
Ecclus. 48. 1–10
or I Kings 19. 1–16
I John 3. 1–3

7 S — THE SEVENTH SUNDAY AFTER TRINITY **(Proper 14)**
Track 1   *Track 2*
Gen. 37. 1–4, 12–28   I Kings 19. 9–18
Ps. 105. 1–6, 16–22, 45b   Ps. 85. 8–13
(*or* 105. 1–10)   Rom. 10. 5–15
Rom. 10. 5–15   Matt. 14. 22–33
G Matt. 14. 22–33
Ps. 88
Song of Sol. 8. 5–7
or I Macc. 14. 4–15
2 Pet. 3. 8–13

8 M — **Dominic, Priest, Founder of the Order of Preachers, 1221**
DEL 19   Com. Religious   *or*   Deut. 10. 12–end
also Ecclus. 39. 1–10   Ps. 147. 13–end
Gw Matt. 17. 22–end
Ps. *1*; 2; 3
Jer. ch. 26
2 Cor. 11. 1–15

9 Tu — **Mary Sumner, Founder of the Mothers' Union, 1921**
Com. Saint   *or*   Deut. 31. 1–8
also Heb. 13. 1–5   Ps. 107. 1–3, 42–end
or Canticle: Deut. 32. 3–4, 7–9
Gw Matt. 18. 1–5, 10, 12–14
Ps. *5*; 6; (8)
Jer. ch. 28
2 Cor. 11. 16–end

10 W — **Laurence, Deacon at Rome, Martyr, 258**
Com. Martyr   *or*   Deut. ch. 34
also 2 Cor. 9. 6–10   Ps. 66. 14–end
Gr Matt. 18. 15–20
Ps. 119. 1–32
Jer. 29. 1–14
2 Cor. ch. 12

11 Th — **Clare of Assisi, Founder of the Minoresses (Poor Clares), 1253**
John Henry Newman, Priest, Tractarian, 1890
Com. Religious   *or*   Josh. 3. 7–11, 13–17
esp. Song of Sol. 8. 6–7   Ps. 114
Gw Matt. 18.21 – 19.1
Ps. 14; *15*; 16
Jer. 30. 1–11
2 Cor. ch. 13

12 F —
Josh. 24. 1–13
Ps. 136. 1–3, 16–22
G Matt. 19. 3–12
Ps. 17; *19*
Jer. 30. 12–22
James 1. 1–11

13 Sa — **Jeremy Taylor, Bishop of Down and Connor, Teacher, 1667**
Florence Nightingale, Nurse, Social Reformer, 1910; Octavia Hill, Social Reformer, 1912
Com. Teacher   *or*   Josh. 24. 14–29
also Titus 2. 7–8, 11–14   Ps. 16. 1, 5–end
Matt. 19. 13–15
Gw
Ps. 20; 21; *23*
Jer. 31. 1–22
James 1. 12–end

14 S — THE EIGHTH SUNDAY AFTER TRINITY **(Proper 15)**
Track 1   *Track 2*
Gen. 45. 1–15   Isa. 56. 1, 6–8
Ps. 133   Ps. 67
Rom. 11. 1–2a, 29–32   Rom. 11. 1–2a, 29–32
Matt. 15. [10–20] 21–28   Matt. 15. [10–20] 21–28
Ps. 92
Jonah ch. 1
or Ecclus. 3. 1–15
2 Pet. 3. 14–end

G

Second Service Evening Prayer		Calendar and Holy Communion	Morning Prayer	Evening Prayer
Ps. *138*; 140; 141 1 Sam. ch. 8 Luke 21. 29–end	G		Esther 6.14 – 7.end 2 Cor. 8.16 – 9.5	1 Sam. ch. 8 Luke 21. 29–end
Ps. 145 1 Sam. 9. 1–14 Luke 22. 1–13 *or First EP of The Transfiguration* Ps. 99; 110 Exod. 24. 12–end John 12. 27–36a ℔ ct	G		Esther ch. 8 2 Cor. 9. 6–end	1 Sam. 9. 1–14 Luke 22. 1–13 *or First EP of The Transfiguration* (Ps. 99; 110) Exod. 24. 12–end John 12. 27–36a ℔ ct
EP: Ps. 72 Exod. 34. 29–end 2 Cor. ch. 3	℔	**THE TRANSFIGURATION OF OUR LORD** Exod. 24. 12–end Ps. 84. 1–7 1 John 3. 1–3 Mark 9. 2–7	(Ps. 27; 150) Ecclus. 48. 1–10 *or 1 Kings 19. 1–16* 2 Pet. 1. 16–19	(Ps. 72) Exod. 34. 29–end 2 Cor. ch. 3
Ps. 86 1 Kings 11.41 – 12.20 Acts 14. 8–20 *Gospel:* John 6. 35, 41–51	G	**THE SEVENTH SUNDAY AFTER TRINITY** 1 Kings 17. 8–16 Ps. 34. 11–end Rom. 6. 19–end Mark 8. 1–10a	Ps. 88 Song of Sol. 8. 5–7 *or 1 Macc. 14. 4–15* 2 Pet. 3. 8–13	Ps. 86 1 Kings 11.41 – 12.20 Acts 14. 8–20
Ps. *4*; 7 1 Sam. 10. 1–16 Luke 22. 24–30	G		Jer. ch. 26 2 Cor. 11. 1–15	1 Sam. 10. 1–16 Luke 22. 24–30
Ps. *9*; 10† 1 Sam. 10. 17–end Luke 22. 31–38	G		Jer. ch. 28 2 Cor. 11. 16–end	1 Sam. 10. 17–end Luke 22. 31–38
Ps. *11*; 12; 13 1 Sam. ch. 11 Luke 22. 39–46	Gr	**Laurence, Deacon at Rome, Martyr, 258** Com. Martyr	Jer. 29. 1–14 2 Cor. ch. 12	1 Sam. ch. 11 Luke 22. 39–46
Ps. 18† 1 Sam. ch. 12 Luke 22. 47–62	G		Jer. 30. 1–11 2 Cor. ch. 13	1 Sam. ch. 12 Luke 22. 47–62
Ps. 22 1 Sam. 13. 5–18 Luke 22. 63–end	G		Jer. 30. 12–22 James 1. 1–11	1 Sam. 13. 5–18 Luke 22. 63–end
Ps. *24*; 25 1 Sam. 13.19 – 14.15 Luke 23. 1–12 ct	G		Jer. 31. 1–22 James 1. 12–end	1 Sam. 13.19 – 14.15 Luke 23. 1–12 ct
Ps. 90 (*or* 90. 1–12) 2 Kings 4. 1–37 Acts 16. 1–15 *Gospel:* John 6. 51–58 *or First EP of The Blessed Virgin Mary* Ps. 72 Prov. 8. 22–31 John 19. 23–27 **W** ct	G	**THE EIGHTH SUNDAY AFTER TRINITY** Jer. 23. 16–24 Ps. 31. 1–6 Rom. 8. 12–17 Matt. 7. 15–21	Ps. 92 Jonah ch. 1 *or Ecclus. 3. 1–15* 2 Pet. 3. 14–end	Ps. 90 (*or* 90. 1–12) 2 Kings 4. 1–37 Acts 16. 1–15

August 2011

			Sunday Principal Service Weekday Eucharist	Third Service Morning Prayer
15 DEL 20	M	**THE BLESSED VIRGIN MARY*** W	Isa. 61. 10–end or Rev. 11.19 – 12.6, 10 Ps. 45. 10–end Gal. 4. 4–7 Luke 1. 46–55	*MP:* Ps. 98; 138; 147. 1–12 Isa. 7. 10–15 Luke 11. 27–28
		or, if The Blessed Virgin Mary is celebrated on 8 September: G	Judg. 2. 11–19 Ps. 106. 34–42 Matt. 19. 16–22	Ps. 27; **30** Jer. 31. 23–25, 27–37 James 2. 1–13
16	Tu G		Judg. 6. 11–24 Ps. 85. 8–end Matt. 19. 23–end	Ps. 32; **36** Jer. 32. 1–15 James 2. 14–end
17	W G		Judg. 9. 6–15 Ps. 21. 1–6 Matt. 20. 1–16	Ps. 34 Jer. 33. 1–13 James ch. 3
18	Th G		Judg. 11. 29–end Ps. 40. 4–11 Matt. 22. 1–14	Ps. 37† Jer. 33. 14–end James 4. 1–12
19	F G		Ruth 1. 1, 3–6, 14–16, 22 Ps. 146 Matt. 22. 34–40	Ps. 31 Jer. ch. 35 James 4.13 – 5.6
20	Sa Gw	**Bernard, Abbot of Clairvaux, Teacher, 1153** *William and Catherine Booth, Founders of the Salvation Army, 1912 and 1890* Com. Religious or *esp.* Rev. 19. 5–9	Ruth 2. 1–3, 8–11; 4. 13–17 Ps. 128 Matt. 23. 1–12	Ps. 41; **42**; 43 Jer. 36. 1–18 James 5. 7–end
21	S G	**THE NINTH SUNDAY AFTER TRINITY (Proper 16)** *Track 1* Exod. 1.8 – 2.10 Ps. 124 Rom. 12. 1–8 Matt. 16. 13–20	*Track 2* Isa. 51. 1–6 Ps. 138 Rom. 12. 1–8 Matt. 16. 13–20	Ps. 104. 1–25 Jonah ch. 2 or Ecclus. 3. 17–29 Rev. ch. 1
22 DEL 21	M G		1 Thess. 1. 1–5, 8–end Ps. 149. 1–5 Matt. 23. 13–22	Ps. 44 Jer. 36. 19–end Mark 1. 1–13
23	Tu G		1 Thess. 2. 1–8 Ps. 139. 1–9 Matt. 23. 23–26	Ps. **48**; 52 Jer. ch. 37 Mark 1. 14–20
24	W R	**BARTHOLOMEW THE APOSTLE**	Isa. 43. 8–13 or Acts 5. 12–16 Ps. 145. 1–7 Acts 5. 12–16 or 1 Cor. 4. 9–15 Luke 22. 24–30	*MP:* Ps. 86; 117 Gen. 28. 10–17 John 1. 43–end
25	Th G		1 Thess. 3. 7–end Ps. 90. 13–end Matt. 24. 42–end	Ps. 56; **57**; (63†) Jer. 38. 14–end Mark 1. 29–end
26	F G		1 Thess. 4. 1–8 Ps. 97 Matt. 25. 1–13	Ps. **51**; 54 Jer. ch. 39 Mark 2. 1–12

*The Blessed Virgin Mary may be celebrated on 8 September instead of 15 August.

Second Service Evening Prayer	Calendar and Holy Communion		Morning Prayer	Evening Prayer
	To celebrate The Blessed Virgin Mary, see *Common Worship* provision.			
EP: Ps. 132 Song of Sol. 2. 1–7 Acts 1. 6–14			Jer. 31. 23–25, 27–37 James 2. 1–13	I Sam. 14. 24–46 Luke 23. 13–25
Ps. 26; **28**; 29 I Sam. 14. 24–46 Luke 23. 13–25		G		
Ps. 33 I Sam. 15. 1–23 Luke 23. 26–43		G	Jer. 32. 1–15 James 2. 14–end	I Sam. 15. 1–23 Luke 23. 26–43
Ps. 119. 33–56 I Sam. ch. 16 Luke 23. 44–56a		G	Jer. 33. 1–13 James ch. 3	I Sam. ch. 16 Luke 23. 44–56a
Ps. 39; **40** I Sam. 17. 1–30 Luke 23.56b – 24.12		G	Jer. 33. 14–end James 4. 1–12	I Sam. 17. 1–30 Luke 23.56b – 24.12
Ps. 35 I Sam. 17. 31–54 Luke 24. 13–35		G	Jer. ch. 35 James 4.13 – 5.6	I Sam. 17. 31–54 Luke 24. 13–35
Ps. 45; **46** I Sam. 17.55 – 18.16 Luke 24. 36–end ct		G	Jer. 36. 1–18 James 5. 7–end	I Sam. 17.55 – 18.16 Luke 24. 36–end ct
	THE NINTH SUNDAY AFTER TRINITY			
Ps. 95 2 Kings 6. 8–23 Acts 17. 15–end *Gospel:* John 6. 56–69	Num. 10.35 – 11.3 Ps. 95 I Cor. 10. 1–13 Luke 16. 1–9 *or* Luke 15. 11–end	G	Ps. 104. 1–25 Jonah ch. 2 *or* Ecclus. 3. 17–29 Rev. ch. 1	Ps. 95 2 Kings 6. 8–23 Acts 17. 15–end
Ps. **47**; 49 I Sam. 19. 1–18 Acts 1. 1–14		G	Jer. 36. 19–end Mark 1. 1–13	I Sam. 19. 1–18 Acts 1. 1–14
Ps. 50 I Sam. 20. 1–17 Acts 1. 15–end *or First EP of Bartholomew* Ps. 97 Isa. 61. 1–9 2 Cor. 6. 1–10 **R** ct		G	Jer. ch. 37 Mark 1. 14–20	I Sam. 20. 1–17 Acts 1. 15–end *or First EP of Bartholomew* (Ps. 97) Isa. 61. 1–9 2 Cor. 6. 1–10 **R** ct
EP: Ps. 91; 116 Ecclus. 39. 1–10 *or* Deut. 18. 15–19 Matt. 10. 1–22	**BARTHOLOMEW THE APOSTLE** Gen. 28. 10–17 Ps. 15 Acts 5. 12–16 Luke 22. 24–30	R	(Ps. 86; 117) Isa. 43. 8–13 John 1. 43–end	(Ps. 91; 116) Ecclus. 39. 1–10 *or* Deut. 18. 15–19 Matt. 10. 1–22
Ps. 61; **62**; 64 I Sam. 21.1 – 22.5 Acts 2. 22–36		G	Jer. 38. 14–end Mark 1. 29–end	I Sam. 21.1 – 22.5 Acts 2. 22–36
Ps. 38 I Sam. 22. 6–end Acts 2. 37–end		G	Jer. ch. 39 Mark 2. 1–12	I Sam. 22. 6–end Acts 2. 37–end

August 2011

			Sunday Principal Service Weekday Eucharist		Third Service Morning Prayer

27 Sa **Monica, Mother of Augustine of Hippo, 387**
Com. Saint *or* 1 Thess. 4. 9–12   Ps. 68
also Ecclus. 26. 1–3, 13–16   Ps. 98. 1–2, 8–end   Jer. ch. 40
Matt. 25. 14–30   Mark 2. 13–22
Gw

28 S **THE TENTH SUNDAY AFTER TRINITY (Proper 17)**
Track 1   *Track 2*
Exod. 3. 1–15   Jer. 15. 15–21   Ps. 107. 1–32
Ps. 105. 1–6, 23–26, 45b   Ps. 26. 1–8   Jonah 3. 1–9
or Ps. 115   Rom. 12. 9–end   *or* Ecclus. 11. [7–18] 19–28
Rom. 12. 9–end   Matt. 16. 21–end   Rev. 3. 14–end
G Matt. 16. 21–end

29 M **The Beheading of John the Baptist**
DEL 22 Jer. 1. 4–10 *or* 1 Thess. 4. 13–end   Ps. 71
Ps. 11   Ps. 96   Jer. ch. 41
Heb. 11.32 – 12.2   Luke 4. 16–30   Mark 2.23 – 3.6
Gr Matt.14. 1–12

30 Tu **John Bunyan, Spiritual Writer, 1688**
Com. Teacher *or* 1 Thess. 5. 1–6, 9–11   Ps. 73
also Heb. 12. 1–2   Ps. 27. 1–8   Jer. ch. 42
Gw Luke 21. 21, 34–36   Luke 4. 31–37   Mark 3. 7–19a

31 W **Aidan, Bishop of Lindisfarne, Missionary, 651**
Com. Missionary *or* Col. 1. 1–8   Ps. 77
also 1 Cor. 9. 16–19   Ps. 34. 11–18   Jer. ch. 43
Gw Luke 4. 38–end   Mark 3. 19b–end

September 2011

1 Th *Giles of Provence, Hermit, c. 710*
Col. 1. 9–14   Ps. 78. 1–39†
Ps. 98. 1–5   Jer. 44. 1–14
G Luke 5. 1–11   Mark 4. 1–20

2 F *The Martyrs of Papua New Guinea, 1901 and 1942*
Col. 1. 15–20   Ps. 55
Ps. 89. 19b–28   Jer. 44. 15–end
G Luke 5. 33–end   Mark 4. 21–34

3 Sa **Gregory the Great, Bishop of Rome, Teacher, 604**
Com. Teacher *or* Col. 1. 21–23   Ps. *76*; 79
also 1 Thess. 2. 3–8   Ps. 117   Jer. ch. 45
Gw Luke 6. 1–5   Mark 4. 35–end

4 S **THE ELEVENTH SUNDAY AFTER TRINITY (Proper 18)**
Track 1   *Track 2*
Exod. 12. 1–14   Ezek. 33. 7–11   Ps. 119. 17–32
Ps. 149   Ps. 119. 33–40   Jonah 3.10 – 4.11
Rom. 13. 8–end   Rom. 13. 8–end   *or* Ecclus. 27.30 – 28.9
G Matt. 18. 15–20   Matt. 18. 15–20   Rev. 8. 1–5

5 M
DEL 23 Col. 1.24 – 2.3   Ps. *80*; 82
Ps. 62. 1–7   Mic. 1. 1–9
G Luke 6. 6–11   Mark 5. 1–20

6 Tu *Allen Gardiner, Founder of the South American Mission Society, 1851*
Col. 2. 6–15   Ps. 87; *89. 1–18*
Ps. 8   Mic. ch. 2
G Luke 6. 12–19   Mark 5. 21–34

7 W
Col. 3. 1–11   Ps. 119. 105–128
Ps. 15   Mic. ch. 3
G Luke 6. 20–26   Mark 5. 35–end

Second Service Evening Prayer		Calendar and Holy Communion	Morning Prayer	Evening Prayer
Ps. 65; *66* 1 Sam. ch. 23 Acts 3. 1–10 ct	G		Jer. ch. 40 Mark 2. 13–22	1 Sam. ch. 23 Acts 3. 1–10 ct
		THE TENTH SUNDAY AFTER TRINITY		
Ps. 105. 1–15 2 Kings 6. 24–25; 7. 3–end Acts 18. 1–16 *Gospel:* Mark 7. 1–8, 14–15, 21–23	G	Jer. 7. 9–15 Ps. 17. 1–8 1 Cor. 12. 1–11 Luke 19. 41–47a	Ps. 107. 1–32 Jonah 3. 1–9 *or* Ecclus. 11. [7–18] 19–28 Rev. 3. 14–end	Ps. 105. 1–15 2 Kings 6. 24–25; 7. 3–end Acts 18. 1–16
Ps. *72*; 75 1 Sam. ch. 24 Acts 3. 11–end	Gr	**The Beheading of John the Baptist** 2 Chron. 24. 17–21 Ps. 92. 11–end Heb. 11.32 – 12.2 Matt. 14. 1–12	Jer. ch. 41 Mark 2.23 – 3.6	1 Sam. ch. 24 Acts 3. 11–end
Ps. 74 1 Sam. ch. 26 Acts 4. 1–12	G		Jer. ch. 42 Mark 3. 7–19a	1 Sam. ch. 26 Acts 4. 1–12
Ps. 119. 81–104 1 Sam. 28. 3–end Acts 4. 13–31	G		Jer. ch. 43 Mark 3. 19b–end	1 Sam. 28. 3–end Acts 4. 13–31
Ps. 78. 40–end† 1 Sam. ch. 31 Acts 4.32 – 5.11	Gw	**Giles of Provence, Hermit, c. 710** Com. Abbot	Jer. 44. 1–14 Mark 4. 1–20	1 Sam. ch. 31 Acts 4.32 – 5.11
Ps. 69 2 Sam. ch. 1 Acts 5. 12–26	G		Jer. 44. 15–end Mark 4. 21–34	2 Sam. ch. 1 Acts 5. 12–26
Ps. 81; *84* 2 Sam. 2. 1–11 Acts 5. 27–end ct	G		Jer. ch. 45 Mark 4. 35–end	2 Sam. 2. 1–11 Acts 5. 27–end ct
		THE ELEVENTH SUNDAY AFTER TRINITY		
Ps. 108; [115] Ezek. 12.21 – 13.16 Acts 19. 1–20 *Gospel:* Mark 7. 24–end	G	1 Kings 3. 5–15 Ps. 28 1 Cor. 15. 1–11 Luke 18. 9–14	Ps. 119. 17–32 Jonah 3.10 – 4.11 *or* Ecclus. 27.30 – 28.9 Rev. 8. 1–5	Ps. 108; [115] Ezek. 12.21 – 13.16 Mark 7. 24–end
Ps. *85*; 86 2 Sam. 3. 12–end Acts ch. 6	G		Mic. 1. 1–9 Mark 5. 1–20	2 Sam. 3. 12–end Acts ch. 6
Ps. 89. 19–end 2 Sam. 5. 1–12 Acts 7. 1–16	G		Mic. ch. 2 Mark 5. 21–34	2 Sam. 5. 1–12 Acts 7. 1–16
Ps. *91*; 93 2 Sam. 6. 1–19 Acts 7. 17–43	Gw	**Evurtius, Bishop of Orleans, 4th century** Com. Bishop	Mic. ch. 3 Mark 5. 35–end	2 Sam. 6. 1–19 Acts 7. 17–43

September 2011

			Sunday Principal Service / Weekday Eucharist	Third Service / Morning Prayer

8 Th — **The Birth of the Blessed Virgin Mary*** — Com. BVM   *or*
Gw

	Sunday Principal Service / Weekday Eucharist	Third Service / Morning Prayer
	Col. 3. 12–17	Ps. 90; **92**
	Ps. 149. 1–5	Mic. 4.1 – 5.1
	Luke 6. 27–38	Mark 6. 1–13

9 F — *Charles Fuge Lowder, Priest, 1880*
G

1 Tim. 1. 1–2, 12–14	Ps. **88**; (95)
Ps. 16	Mic. 5. 2–end
Luke 6. 39–42	Mark 6. 14–29

10 Sa — *Track 1*
G

1 Tim. 1. 15–17	Ps. 96; **97**; 100
Ps. 113	Mic. ch. 6
Luke 6. 43–end	Mark 6. 30–44

11 S — THE TWELFTH SUNDAY AFTER TRINITY **(Proper 19)**
Track 1 / *Track 2*
G

Track 1	Track 2	Third Service / Morning Prayer
Exod. 14. 19–end	Gen. 50. 15–21	Ps. 119. 65–88
Ps. 114	Ps. 103. 1–13 (or 103. 8–13)	Isa. 44.24 – 45.8
or Canticle: Exod. 15. 1b–11, 20–21	Rom. 14. 1–12	Rev. 12. 1–12
Rom. 14. 1–12	Matt. 18. 21–35	
Matt. 18. 21–35		

12 M
DEL 24   G

1 Tim. 2. 1–8	Ps. **98**; 99; 101
Ps. 28	Mic. 7. 1–7
Luke 7. 1–10	Mark 6. 45–end

13 Tu — **John Chrysostom, Bishop of Constantinople, Teacher, 407**
Com. Teacher   *or*
esp. Matt. 5. 13–19
also Jer. 1. 4–10

Gw

1 Tim. 3. 1–13	Ps. 106† (or Ps. 103)
Ps. 101	Mic. 7. 8–end
Luke 7. 11–17	Mark 7. 1–13

14 W — HOLY CROSS DAY
R

Num. 21. 4–9	MP: Ps. 2; 8; 146
Ps. 22. 23–28	Gen. 3. 1–15
Phil. 2. 6–11	John 12. 27–36a
John 3. 13–17	

15 Th — **Cyprian, Bishop of Carthage, Martyr, 258**
Com. Martyr   *or*
esp. 1 Pet. 4. 12–end
Gr   *also* Matt. 18. 18–22

1 Tim. 4. 12–end	Ps. 113; **115**
Ps. 111. 6–end	Hab. 1.12 – 2.5
Luke 7. 36–end	Mark 7. 24–30

16 F — **Ninian, Bishop of Galloway, Apostle of the Picts, c. 432**
Edward Bouverie Pusey, Priest, Tractarian, 1882
Com. Missionary   *or*
esp. Acts 13. 46–49
Gw   Mark 16. 15–end

1 Tim. 6. 2b–12	Ps. 139
Ps. 49. 1–9	Hab. 2. 6–end
Luke 8. 1–3	Mark 7. 31–end

17 Sa — **Hildegard, Abbess of Bingen, Visionary, 1179**
Com. Religious   *or*
also 1 Cor. 2. 9–13
Luke 10. 21–24
Gw

1 Tim. 6. 13–16	Ps. 120; **121**; 122
Ps. 100	Hab. 3. 2–19a
Luke 8. 4–15	Mark 8. 1–10

18 S — THE THIRTEENTH SUNDAY AFTER TRINITY **(Proper 20)**
Track 1 / *Track 2*
G

Track 1	Track 2	Third Service / Morning Prayer
Exod. 16. 2–15	Jonah 3.10 – 4.end	Ps. 119. 153–end
Ps. 105. 1–6, 37–end	Ps. 145. 1–8	Isa. 45. 9–22
(or 105. 37–end)	Phil. 1. 21–end	Rev. 14. 1–5
Phil. 1. 21–end	Matt. 20. 1–16	
Matt. 20. 1–16		

*The Blessed Virgin Mary may be celebrated on 8 September instead of 15 August.

Second Service Evening Prayer		Calendar and Holy Communion	Morning Prayer	Evening Prayer
Ps. 94 2 Sam. 7. 1–17 Acts 7. 44–53	Gw	**The Birth of the Blessed Virgin Mary** Gen. 3. 9–15 Ps. 45. 11–18 Rom. 5. 12–17 Luke 11. 27–28	Mic. 4.1 – 5.1 Mark 6. 1–13	2 Sam. 7. 1–17 Acts 7. 44–53
Ps. 102 2 Sam. 7. 18–end Acts 7.54 – 8.3	G		Mic. 5. 2–end Mark 6. 14–29	2 Sam. 7. 18–end Acts 7.54 – 8.3
Ps. 104 2 Sam. ch. 9 Acts 8. 4–25 ct	G		Mic. ch. 6 Mark 6. 30–44	2 Sam. ch. 9 Acts 8. 4–25 ct
	G	THE TWELFTH SUNDAY AFTER TRINITY		
Ps. 119. 41–48 [49–64] Ezek. 20. 1–8, 33–44 Acts 20. 17–end *Gospel*: Mark 8. 27–end	G	Exod. 34. 29–end Ps. 34. 1–10 2 Cor. 3. 4–9 Mark 7. 31–37	Ps. 119. 65–88 Isa. 44.24 – 45.8 Rev. 12. 1–12	Ps. 119. 41–48 [49–64] Ezek. 20. 1–8, 33–44 Acts 20. 17–end
Ps. *105*† (or 103) 2 Sam. ch. 11 Acts 8. 26–end	G		Mic. 7. 1–7 Mark 6. 45–end	2 Sam. ch. 11 Acts 8. 26–end
Ps. 107† 2 Sam. 12. 1–25 Acts 9. 1–19a *or First EP of Holy Cross Day* Ps. 66 Isa. 52.13 – 53.end Eph. 2. 11–end **R** ct	G		Mic. 7. 8–end Mark 7. 1–13	2 Sam. 12. 1–25 Acts 9. 1–19a
EP: Ps. 110; 150 Isa. 63. 1–16 1 Cor. 1. 18–25	Gr	**Holy Cross Day** To celebrate Holy Cross as a festival, see *Common Worship* provision. Num. 21. 4–9 Ps. 67 1 Cor. 1. 17–25 John 12. 27–33	Hab. 1. 1–11 Mark 7. 14–23	2 Sam. 15. 1–12 Acts 9. 19b–31
Ps. 114; *116*; 117 2 Sam. 15. 13–end Acts 9. 32–end	G		Hab. 1.12 – 2.5 Mark 7. 24–30	2 Sam. 15. 13–end Acts 9. 32–end
Ps. *130*; 131; 137 2 Sam. 16. 1–14 Acts 10. 1–16	G		Hab. 2. 6–end Mark 7. 31–end	2 Sam. 16. 1–14 Acts 10. 1–16
Ps. 118 2 Sam. 17. 1–23 Acts 10. 17–33 ct	Gr	**Lambert, Bishop of Maastricht, Martyr, 709** Com. Martyr	Hab. 3. 2–19a Mark 8. 1–10	2 Sam. 17. 1–23 Acts 10. 17–33 ct
	G	THE THIRTEENTH SUNDAY AFTER TRINITY		
Ps. 119. 113–136 (or 119. 121–128) Ezek. 33.23, 30 – 34.10 Acts 26. 1, 9–25 *Gospel*: Mark 9. 30–37	G	Lev. 19. 13–18 Ps. 74. 20–end Gal. 3. 16–22 *or* Heb. 13. 1–6 Luke 10. 23b–37	Ps. 119. 153–end Isa. 45. 9–22 Rev. 14. 1–5	Ps. 119. 113–136 (or 119. 121–128) Ezek. 33.23, 30 – 34.10 Acts 26. 1, 9–25

September 2011

			Sunday Principal Service Weekday Eucharist	Third Service Morning Prayer

19
DEL 25

M		*Theodore of Tarsus, Archbishop of Canterbury, 690*		
			Ezra 1. 1–6	Ps. 123; 124; 125; *126*
			Ps. 126	Hag. 1. 1–11
G			Luke 8. 16–18	Mark 8. 11–21

20

Tu		**John Coleridge Patteson, first Bishop of Melanesia, and his Companions, Martyrs, 1871**		
		Com. Martyr	*or* Ezra 6. 7–8, 12, 14–20	Ps. *132*; 133
		esp. 2 Chron. 24. 17–21	Ps. 124	Hag. 1.12 – 2.9
		also Acts 7. 55–end	Luke 8. 19–21	Mark 8. 22–26
Gr				

21

W		MATTHEW, APOSTLE AND EVANGELIST		
			Prov. 3. 13–18	MP: Ps. 49; 117
			Ps. 119. 65–72	1 Kings 19. 15–end
			2 Cor. 4. 1–6	2 Tim. 3. 14–end
R			Matt. 9. 9–13	

22

Th			Hag. 1. 1–8	Ps. *143*; 146
			Ps. 149. 1–5	Zech. 1. 1–17
G			Luke 9. 7–9	Mark 9. 2–13

23

F			Hag. 1.15b – 2.9	Ps. 142; *144*
			Ps. 43	Zech. 1.18 – 2.end
G			Luke 9. 18–22	Mark 9. 14–29

24

Sa			Zech. 2. 1–5, 10–11	Ps. 147
			Ps. 125	Zech. ch. 3
			or Canticle: Jer. 31. 10–13	Mark 9. 30–37
G			Luke 9. 43b–45	

25

S		THE FOURTEENTH SUNDAY AFTER TRINITY **(Proper 21)**		
		Track 1	Track 2	
		Exod. 17. 1–7	Ezek. 18. 1–4, 25–end	Ps. 125; 126; 127
		Ps. 78. 1–4, 12–16 (or 78. 1–7)	Ps. 25. 1–8	Isa. 48. 12–21
		Phil. 2. 1–13	Phil. 2. 1–13	Luke 11. 37–54
G		Matt. 21. 23–32	Matt. 21. 23–32	

26
DEL 26

M		*Wilson Carlile, Founder of the Church Army, 1942*		
			Zech. 8. 1–18	Ps. *1*; 2; 3
			Ps. 102. 12–22	Zech. ch. 4
G			Luke 9. 46–50	Mark 9. 38–end

27

Tu		**Vincent de Paul, Founder of the Congregation of the Mission (Lazarists), 1660**		
		Com. Religious	*or* Zech. 8. 20–end	Ps. *5*; 6; (8)
		also 1 Cor. 1. 25–end	Ps. 87	Zech. 6. 9–end
Gw		Matt. 25. 34–40	Luke 9. 51–56	Mark 10. 1–16

28

W		Ember Day*		
			Neh. 2. 1–8	Ps. 119. 1–32
			Ps. 137. 1–6	Zech. ch. 7
			Luke 9. 57–end	Mark 10. 17–31
G *or* R				

29

Th		MICHAEL AND ALL ANGELS		
			Gen. 28. 10–17	MP: Ps. 34; 150
			or Rev. 12. 7–12	Tobit 12. 6–end
			Ps. 103. 19–end	*or* Dan. 12. 1–4
			Rev. 12. 7–12	Acts 12. 1–11
			or Heb. 1. 5–end	
W			John 1. 47–end	

*For Ember Day provision, see p. 13.

Second Service Evening Prayer	Calendar and Holy Communion		Morning Prayer	Evening Prayer
Ps. *127*; 128; 129 2 Sam. 18. 1–18 Acts 10. 34–end		G	Hag. 1. 1–11 Mark 8. 11–21	2 Sam. 18. 1–18 Acts 10. 34–end
Ps. (134); *135* 2 Sam. 18.19 – 19.8a Acts 11. 1–18 *or First EP of Matthew* Ps. 34 Isa. 33. 13–17 Matt. 6. 19–end **R ct**		G	Hag. 1.12 – 2.9 Mark 8. 22–26	2 Sam. 18.19 – 19.8a Acts 11. 1–18 *or First EP of Matthew* (Ps. 34) Prov. 3. 3–18 Matt. 6. 19–end **R ct**
EP: Ps. 119. 33–40, 89–96 Eccles. 5. 4–12 Matt. 19. 16–end	**MATTHEW, APOSTLE AND EVANGELIST** Ember Day Isa. 33. 13–17 Ps. 119. 65–72 2 Cor. 4. 1–6 Matt. 9. 9–13	R	(Ps. 49; 117) 1 Kings 19. 15–end 2 Tim. 3. 14–end	(Ps. 119. 33–40, 89–96) Eccles. 5. 4–12 Matt. 19. 16–end
Ps. *138*; 140; 141 2 Sam. 19. 24–end Acts 12. 1–17		G	Zech. 1. 1–17 Mark 9. 2–13	2 Sam. 19. 24–end Acts 12. 1–17
Ps. 145 2 Sam. 23. 1–7 Acts 12. 18–end	Ember Day Ember CEG	G	Zech. 1.18 – 2.end Mark 9. 14–29	2 Sam. 23. 1–7 Acts 12. 18–end
Ps. *148*; 149; 150 2 Sam. ch. 24 Acts 13. 1–12 ct	Ember Day Ember CEG	G	Zech. ch. 3 Mark 9. 30–37	2 Sam. ch. 24 Acts 13. 1–12 ct
Ps. [120; 123]; 124 Ezek. 37. 15–end 1 John 2. 22–end *Gospel*: Mark 9. 38–end	**THE FOURTEENTH SUNDAY AFTER TRINITY** 2 Kings 5. 9–16 Ps. 118. 1–9 Gal. 5. 16–24 Luke 17. 11–19	G	Ps. 125; 126; 127 Isa. 48. 12–21 Luke 11. 37–54	Ps. [120; 123]; 124 Ezek. 37. 15–end 1 John 2. 22–end
Ps. *4*; 7 1 Kings 1. 5–31 Acts 13. 13–43	**Cyprian, Bishop of Carthage, Martyr, 258** Com. Martyr	Gr	Zech. ch. 4 Mark 9. 38–end	1 Kings 1. 5–31 Acts 13. 13–43
Ps. *9*; 10† 1 Kings 1.32 – 2.4, 10–12 Acts 13.44 – 14.7		G	Zech. 6. 9–end Mark 10. 1–16	1 Kings 1.32 – 2.4, 10–12 Acts 13.44 – 14.7
Ps. *11*; 12; 13 1 Kings ch. 3 Acts 14. 8–end *or First EP of Michael and All Angels* Ps. 91 2 Kings 6. 8–17 Matt. 18. 1–6, 10 **W ct**		G	Zech. ch. 7 Mark 10. 17–31	1 Kings ch. 3 Acts 14. 8–end *or First EP of Michael and All Angels* (Ps. 91) 2 Kings 6. 8–17 John 1. 47–51 **W ct**
EP: Ps. 138; 148 Dan. 10. 4–end Rev. ch. 5	**MICHAEL AND ALL ANGELS** Dan. 10. 10–19a Ps. 103. 17–22 Rev. 12. 7–12 Matt. 18. 1–10	W	(Ps. 34; 150) Tobit 12. 6–end *or* Dan. 12. 1–4 Acts 12. 1–11	(Ps. 138; 148) Gen. 28. 10–17 Rev. ch. 5

September 2011

			Sunday Principal Service Weekday Eucharist	Third Service Morning Prayer
30	F **G** *or* **R**	*Jerome, Translator of the Scriptures, Teacher, 420* Ember Day*	Baruch 1. 15–end *or* Deut. 31. 7–13 Ps. 79. 1–9 Luke 10. 13–16	Ps. 17; ***19*** Zech. 8. 9–end Mark 10. 35–45

October 2011

1	Sa **G** *or* **R**	*Remigius, Bishop of Rheims, Apostle of the Franks, 533; Anthony Ashley Cooper, Earl of Shaftesbury, Social Reformer, 1885* Ember Day*	Baruch 4. 5–12, 27–29 *or* Josh. 22. 1–6 Ps. 69. 33–37 Luke 10. 17–24	Ps. 20; 21; ***23*** Zech. 9. 1–12 Mark 10. 46–end
2	S **G**	THE FIFTEENTH SUNDAY AFTER TRINITY **(Proper 22)** *Track 1* Exod. 20. 1–4, 7–9, 12–20 Ps. 19 (*or* 19. 7–end) Phil. 3. 4b–14 Matt. 21. 33–end	*Track 2* Isa. 5. 1–7 Ps. 80. 9–17 Phil. 3. 4b–14 Matt. 21. 33–end	Ps. 128; 129; 134 Isa. 49. 13–23 Luke 12. 1–12
	𝔚	*or, if observed as Dedication Festival*:	1 Kings 8. 22–30 *or* Rev. 21. 9–14 Ps. 122 Heb. 12. 18–24 Matt. 21. 12–16	*MP*: Ps. 48; 150 Hag. 2. 6–9 Heb. 10. 19–25
3 DEL 27	M **G**		Jonah 1.1 – 2.2, 10 *Canticle*: Jonah 2. 2–4, 7 *or* Ps. 69. 1–6 Luke 10. 25–37	Ps. 27; ***30*** Zech. ch. 10 Mark 11. 1–11
4	Tu **Gw**	**Francis of Assisi, Friar, Founder of the Friars Minor, 1226** Com. Religious *or* *also* Gal. 6. 14–end Luke 12. 22–34	Jonah ch. 3 Ps. 130 Luke 10. 38–end	Ps. 32; ***36*** Zech. 11. 4–end Mark 11. 12–26
5	W **G**		Jonah ch. 4 Ps. 86. 1–9 Luke 11. 1–4	Ps. 34 Zech. 12. 1–10 Mark 11. 27–end
6	Th **Gr**	**William Tyndale, Translator of the Scriptures, Reformation Martyr, 1536** Com. Martyr *or* *also* Prov. 8. 4–11 2 Tim. 3. 12–end	Mal. 3.13 – 4.2a Ps. 1 Luke 11. 5–13	Ps. 37† Zech. ch. 13 Mark 12. 1–12
7	F **G**		Joel 1. 13–15; 2. 1–2 Ps. 9. 1–7 Luke 11. 15–26	Ps. 31 Zech. 14. 1–11 Mark 12. 13–17
8	Sa **G**		Joel 3. 12–end Ps. 97. 1, 8–end Luke 11. 27–28	Ps. 41; ***42***; 43 Zech. 14. 12–end Mark 12. 18–27
9	S **G**	THE SIXTEENTH SUNDAY AFTER TRINITY **(Proper 23)** *Track 1* Exod. 32. 1–14 Ps. 106. 1–6, 19–23 (*or* 106. 1–6) Phil. 4. 1–9 Matt. 22. 1–14	*Track 2* Isa. 25. 1–9 Ps. 23 Phil. 4. 1–9 Matt. 22. 1–14	Ps. 138; 141 Isa. 50. 4–10 Luke 13. 22–30

*For Ember Day provision, see p. 13.

Second Service Evening Prayer		Calendar and Holy Communion	Morning Prayer	Evening Prayer
		Jerome, Translator of the Scriptures, Teacher, 420 Com. Doctor		
Ps. 22 I Kings 6. 1, 11–28 Acts 15. 22–35	Gw		Zech. 8. 9–end Mark 10. 35–45	I Kings 6. 1, 11–28 Acts 15. 22–35
		Remigius, Bishop of Rheims, Apostle of the Franks, 533 Com. Bishop		
Ps. *24*; 25 I Kings 8. 1–30 Acts 15.36 – 16.5 ct or First EP of Dedication Festival Ps. 24 2 Chron. 7. 11–16 John 4. 19–29 ℣ ct	Gw		Zech. 9. 1–12 Mark 10. 46–end	I Kings 8. 1–30 Acts 15.36 – 16.5 ct or First EP of Dedication Festival Ps. 24 2 Chron. 7. 11–16 John 4. 19–29 ℣ ct
		THE FIFTEENTH SUNDAY AFTER TRINITY		
Ps. 136 (or 136. 1–9) Prov. 2. 1–11 I John 2. 1–17 *Gospel:* Mark 10. 2–16	G	Josh. 24. 14–25 Ps. 92. 1–6 Gal. 6. 11–end Matt. 6. 24–end	Ps. 128; 129; 134 Isa. 49. 13–23 Luke 12. 1–12	Ps. 136 (or 136. 1–9) Prov. 2. 1–11 I John 2. 1–17
EP: Ps. 132 Jer. 7. 1–11 I Cor. 3. 9–17 *Gospel:* Luke 19. 1–10	℣	*or, if observed as Dedication Festival:* 2 Chron. 7. 11–16 Ps. 122 I Cor. 3. 9–17 *or* I Pet. 2. 1–5 Matt. 21. 12–16 *or* John 10. 22–29	Ps. 48; 150 Hag. 2. 6–9 Heb. 10. 19–25	Ps. 132 Jer. 7. 1–11 Luke 19. 1–10
Ps. 26; *28*; 29 I Kings 8. 31–62 Acts 16. 6–24	G		Zech. ch. 10 Mark 11. 1–11	I Kings 8. 31–62 Acts 16. 6–24
Ps. 33 I Kings 8.63 – 9.9 Acts 16. 25–end	G		Zech. 11. 4–end Mark 11. 12–26	I Kings 8.63 – 9.9 Acts 16. 25–end
Ps. 119. 33–56 I Kings 10. 1–25 Acts 17. 1–15	G		Zech. 12. 1–10 Mark 11. 27–end	I Kings 10. 1–25 Acts 17. 1–15
Ps. 39; *40* I Kings 11. 1–13 Acts 17. 16–end	Gr	**Faith of Aquitaine, Martyr, c. 304** Com. Virgin Martyr	Zech. ch. 13 Mark 12. 1–12	I Kings 11. 1–13 Acts 17. 16–end
Ps. 35 I Kings 11.26–end Acts 18. 1–21	G		Zech. 14. 1–11 Mark 12. 13–17	I Kings 11.26–end Acts 18. 1–21
Ps. 45; *46* I Kings 12. 1–24 Acts 18.22 – 19.7 ct	G		Zech. 14. 12–end Mark 12. 18–27	I Kings 12. 1–24 Acts 18.22 – 19.7 ct
		THE SIXTEENTH SUNDAY AFTER TRINITY		
Ps. 139. 1–18 (or 139. 1–11) Prov. 3. 1–18 I John 3. 1–15 *Gospel:* Mark 10. 17–31	G	I Kings 17. 17–end Ps. 102. 12–17 Eph. 3. 13–end Luke 7. 11–17	Ps. 138; 141 Isa. 50. 4–10 Luke 13. 22–30	Ps. 139. 1–18 (or 139. 1–11) Prov. 3. 1–18 I John 3. 1–15

October 2011

			Sunday Principal Service Weekday Eucharist	Third Service Morning Prayer
10 DEL 28	M	**Paulinus, Bishop of York, Missionary, 644** *Thomas Traherne, Poet, Spiritual Writer, 1674* Com. Missionary *or* *esp.* Matt. 28. 16–end	Rom. 1. 1–7 Ps. 98 Luke 11. 29–32	Ps. 44 Ecclus. 1. 1–10 or Ezek. 1. 1–14
	Gw			Mark 12. 28–34
11	Tu	*Ethelburga, Abbess of Barking, 675; James the Deacon, Companion of Paulinus, 7th century* 	Rom. 1. 16–25 Ps. 19. 1–4 Luke 11. 37–41	Ps. *48*; 52 Ecclus. 1. 11–end or Ezek. 1.15 – 2.2
	G			Mark 12. 35–end
12	W	**Wilfrid of Ripon, Bishop, Missionary, 709** *Elizabeth Fry, Prison Reformer, 1845; Edith Cavell, Nurse, 1915* Com. Missionary *or* *esp.* Luke 5. 1–11 *also* 1 Cor. 1. 18–25	Rom. 2. 1–11 Ps. 62. 1–8 Luke 11. 42–46	Ps. 119. 57–80 Ecclus. ch. 2 or Ezek. 2.3 – 3.11
	Gw			Mark 13. 1–13
13	Th	**Edward the Confessor, King of England, 1066** Com. Saint *or* *also* 2 Sam. 23. 1–5 1 John 4. 13–16	Rom. 3. 21–30 Ps. 130 Luke 11. 47–end	Ps. 56; *57*; (63†) Ecclus. 3. 17–29 or Ezek. 3. 12–end
	Gw			Mark 13. 14–23
14	F		Rom. 4. 1–8 Ps. 32 Luke 12. 1–7	Ps. *51*; 54 Ecclus. 4. 11–28 or Ezek. ch. 8
	G			Mark 13. 24–31
15	Sa	**Teresa of Avila, Teacher, 1582** Com. Teacher *or* *also* Rom. 8. 22–27	Rom. 4. 13, 16–18 Ps. 105. 6–10, 41–44 Luke 12. 8–12	Ps. 68 Ecclus. 4.29 – 6.1 or Ezek. ch. 9
	Gw			Mark 13. 32–end
16	S	**THE SEVENTEENTH SUNDAY AFTER TRINITY (Proper 24)** *Track 1* Exod. 33. 12–end Ps. 99 1 Thess. 1. 1–10	*Track 2* Isa. 45. 1–7 Ps. 96. 1–9 [10–13] 1 Thess. 1. 1–10	Ps. 145; 149 Isa. 54. 1–14 Luke 13. 31–end
	G	Matt. 22. 15–22	Matt. 22. 15–22	
17 DEL 29	M	**Ignatius, Bishop of Antioch, Martyr, c. 107** Com. Martyr *or* *also* Phil. 3. 7–12 John 6. 52–58	Rom. 4. 20–end Canticle: Benedictus 1–6 Luke 12. 13–21	Ps. 71 Ecclus. 6. 14–end or Ezek. 10. 1–19 Mark 14. 1–11
	Gr			
18	Tu	LUKE THE EVANGELIST	Isa. 35. 3–6 or Acts 16. 6–12a Ps. 147. 1–7 2 Tim. 4. 5–17	MP: Ps. 145; 146 Isa. ch. 55 Luke 1. 1–4
	R		Luke 10. 1–9	
19	W	**Henry Martyn, Translator of the Scriptures, Missionary in India and Persia, 1812** Com. Missionary *or* *esp.* Mark 16. 15–end *also* Isa. 55. 6–11	Rom. 6. 12–18 Ps. 124 Luke 12. 39–48	Ps. 77 Ecclus. 10. 6–8, 12–24 or Ezek. 12. 1–16
	Gw			Mark 14. 26–42
20	Th		Rom. 6. 19–end Ps. 1 Luke 12. 49–53	Ps. 78. 1–39† Ecclus. 11. 7–28 or Ezek. 12. 17–end
	G			Mark 14. 43–52

Second Service Evening Prayer		Calendar and Holy Communion	Morning Prayer	Evening Prayer
Ps. *47*; 49 1 Kings 12.25 – 13.10 Acts 19. 8–20	G		Ecclus. 1. 1–10 or Ezek. 1. 1–14 Mark 12. 28–34	1 Kings 12.25 – 13.10 Acts 19. 8–20
Ps. 50 1 Kings 13. 11–end Acts 19. 21–end	G		Ecclus. 1. 11–end or Ezek. 1.15 – 2.2 Mark 12. 35–end	1 Kings 13. 11–end Acts 19. 21–end
Ps. *59*; 60; (67) 1 Kings ch. 17 Acts 20. 1–16	G		Ecclus. ch. 2 or Ezek. 2.3 – 3.11 Mark 13. 1–13	1 Kings ch. 17 Acts 20. 1–16
Ps. 61; *62*; 64 1 Kings 18. 1–20 Acts 20. 17–end	Gw	**Edward the Confessor, King of England, 1066, translated 1163** Com. Saint	Ecclus. 3. 17–29 or Ezek. 3. 12–end Mark 13. 14–23	1 Kings 18. 1–20 Acts 20. 17–end
Ps. 38 1 Kings 18. 21–end Acts 21. 1–16	G		Ecclus. 4. 11–28 or Ezek. ch. 8 Mark 13. 24–31	1 Kings 18. 21–end Acts 21. 1–16
Ps. 65; *66* 1 Kings ch. 19 Acts 21. 17–36 ct	G		Ecclus. 4.29 – 6.1 or Ezek. ch. 9 Mark 13. 32–end	1 Kings ch. 19 Acts 21. 17–36 ct
Ps. 142 [143. 1–11] Prov. 4. 1–18 1 John 3.16 – 4.6 *Gospel:* Mark 10. 35–45	G	**THE SEVENTEENTH SUNDAY AFTER TRINITY** Prov. 25. 6–14 Ps. 33. 6–12 Eph. 4. 1–6 Luke 14. 1–11	Ps. 138 Isa. 54. 1–14 Luke 13. 31–end	Ps. 142 [143. 1–11] Prov. 4. 1–18 1 John 3.16 – 4.6
Ps. *72*; 75 1 Kings ch. 21 Acts 21.37 – 22.21 *or First EP of Luke* Ps. 33 Hos. 6. 1–3 2 Tim. 3. 10–end **R ct**	Gw	**Etheldreda, Abbess of Ely, 679** Com. Abbess	Ecclus. 6. 14–end or Ezek. 10. 1–19 Mark 14. 1–11	1 Kings ch. 21 Acts 21.37 – 22.21 *or First EP of Luke* (Ps. 33) Hos. 6. 1–3 2 Tim. 3. 10–end **R ct**
EP: Ps. 103 Ecclus. 38. 1–14 *or* Isa. 61. 1–6 Col. 4. 7–end	R	**LUKE THE EVANGELIST** Isa. 35. 3–6 Ps. 147. 1–6 2 Tim. 4. 5–15 Luke 10. 1–9 *or* Luke 7. 36–end	(Ps. 145; 146) Isa. ch. 55 Luke 1. 1–4	(Ps. 103) Ecclus. 38. 1–14 *or* Isa. 61. 1–6 Col. 4. 7–end
Ps. 119. 81–104 1 Kings 22. 29–45 Acts 23. 12–end	G		Ecclus. 10. 6–8, 12–24 or Ezek. 12. 1–16 Mark 14. 26–42	1 Kings 22. 29–45 Acts 23. 12–end
Ps. 78. 40–end† 2 Kings 1. 2–17 Acts 24. 1–23	G		Ecclus. 11. 7–28 or Ezek. 12. 17–end Mark 14. 43–52	2 Kings 1. 2–17 Acts 24. 1–23

October 2011

			Sunday Principal Service Weekday Eucharist	Third Service Morning Prayer
21	F G		Rom. 7. 18–end Ps. 119. 33–40 Luke 12. 54–end	Ps. 55 Ecclus. 14.20 – 15.10 or Ezek. 13. 1–16 Mark 14. 53–65
22	Sa G		Rom. 8. 1–11 Ps. 24. 1–6 Luke 13. 1–9	Ps. **76**; 79 Ecclus. 15. 11–end or Ezek. 14. 1–11 Mark 14. 66–end
23	S G	THE LAST SUNDAY AFTER TRINITY* *Track 1* Deut. 34. 1–12 Ps. 90. 1–6, 13–17 (or 90. 1–6) 1 Thess. 2. 1–8 Matt. 22. 34–end *or, if being observed as Bible Sunday:*	*Track 2* Lev. 19. 1–2, 15–18 Ps. 1 1 Thess. 2. 1–8 Matt. 22. 34–end Neh. 8. 1–4a [5–6] 8–12 Ps. 119. 9–16 Col. 3. 12–17 Matt. 24. 30–35	Ps. 119. 137–152 Isa. 59. 9–20 Luke 14. 1–14 Ps. 119. 137–152 Deut. 17. 14–15, 18–end John 5. 36b–end
	G			
24 DEL 30	M G		Rom. 8. 12–17 Ps. 68. 1–6, 19 Luke 13. 10–17	Ps. **80**; 82 Ecclus. 16. 17–end or Ezek. 14. 12–end Mark 15. 1–15
25	Tu G	*Crispin and Crispinian, Martyrs at Rome, c. 287*	Rom. 8. 18–25 Ps. 126 Luke 13. 18–21	Ps. 87; **89.** *1–18* Ecclus. 17. 1–24 or Ezek. 18. 1–20 Mark 15. 16–32
26	W Gw	**Alfred the Great, King of the West Saxons, Scholar, 899** *Cedd, Abbot of Lastingham, Bishop of the East Saxons, 664*** Com. Saint or *also* 2 Sam. 23. 1–5 John 18. 33–37	Rom. 8. 26–30 Ps. 13 Luke 13. 22–30	Ps. 119. 105–128 Ecclus. 18. 1–14 or Ezek. 18. 21–32 Mark 15. 33–41
27	Th G		Rom. 8. 31–end Ps. 109. 20–26, 29–30 Luke 13. 31–end	Ps. 90; **92** Ecclus. 19. 4–17 or Ezek. 20. 1–20 Mark 15. 42–end
28	F R	SIMON AND JUDE, APOSTLES	Isa. 28. 14–16 Ps. 119. 89–96 Eph. 2. 19–end John 15. 17–end	MP: Ps. 116; 117 Wisd. 5. 1–16 or Isa. 45. 18–end Luke 6. 12–16
29	Sa Gr	**James Hannington, Bishop of Eastern Equatorial Africa, Martyr in Uganda, 1885** Com. Martyr or *esp.* Matt. 10. 28–39	Rom. 11. 1–2, 11–12, 25–29 Ps. 94. 14–19 Luke 14. 1, 7–11	Ps. 96; **97**; 100 Ecclus. 21. 1–17 or Ezek. 24. 15–end Mark 16. 9–end

*If the Dedication Festival is kept on this Sunday, use the provision given on 1 and 2 October.
**Chad may be celebrated with Cedd on 26 October instead of 2 March.

Second Service Evening Prayer	Calendar and Holy Communion		Morning Prayer	Evening Prayer
Ps. 69 2 Kings 2. 1–18 Acts 24.24 – 25.12		G	Ecclus. 14.20 – 15.10 or Ezek. 13. 1–16 Mark 14. 53–65	2 Kings 2. 1–18 Acts 24.24 – 25.12
Ps. 81; *84* 2 Kings 4. 1–37 Acts 25. 13–end ct		G	Ecclus. 15. 11–end or Ezek. 14. 1–11 Mark 14. 66–end	2 Kings 4. 1–37 Acts 25. 13–end ct
	THE EIGHTEENTH SUNDAY AFTER TRINITY			
Ps. 119. 89–104 Eccles. chs 11 & 12 2 Tim. 2. 1–7 *Gospel:* Mark 12. 28–34 Ps. 119. 89–104 Isa. 55. 1–11 Luke 4. 14–30	Deut. 6. 4–9 Ps. 122 1 Cor. 1. 4–8 Matt. 22. 34–end	G	Ps. 119. 137–152 Isa. 59. 9–20 Luke 14. 11–24	Ps. 119. 89–104 Eccles. chs 11 & 12 2 Tim. 2. 1–7
Ps. *85*; 86 2 Kings ch. 5 Acts 26. 1–23		G	Ecclus. 16. 17–end or Ezek. 14. 12–end Mark 15. 1–15	2 Kings ch. 5 Acts 26. 1–23
Ps. 89. 19–end 2 Kings 6. 1–23 Acts 26. 24–end	**Crispin, Martyr at Rome, c. 287** Com. Martyr	Gr	Ecclus. 17. 1–24 or Ezek. 18. 1–20 Mark 15. 16–32	2 Kings 6. 1–23 Acts 26. 24–end
Ps. *91*; 93 2 Kings 9. 1–16 Acts 27. 1–26		G	Ecclus. 18. 1–14 or Ezek. 18. 21–32 Mark 15. 33–41	2 Kings 9. 1–16 Acts 27. 1–26
Ps. 94 2 Kings 9. 17–end Acts 27. 27–end *or First EP of Simon and Jude* Ps. 124; 125; 126 Deut. 32. 1–4 John 14. 15–26 **R ct**		G	Ecclus. 19. 4–17 or Ezek. 20. 1–20 Mark 15. 42–end	2 Kings 9. 17–end Acts 27. 27–end *or First EP of Simon and Jude* (Ps. 124; 125; 126) Deut. 32. 1–4 John 14. 15–26 **R ct**
EP: Ps. 119. 1–16 1 Macc. 2. 42–66 *or* Jer. 3. 11–18 Jude 1–4, 17–end	**SIMON AND JUDE, APOSTLES** Isa. 28. 9–16 Ps. 116. 11–end Jude 1–8 *or* Rev. 21. 9–14 John 15. 17–end	R	(Ps. 119. 89–96) Wisd. 5. 1–16 *or* Isa. 45. 18–end Luke 6. 12–16	(Ps. 119. 1–16) 1 Macc. 2. 42–66 *or* Jer. 3. 11–18 Eph. 2. 19–end
Ps. 104 2 Kings 17. 1–23 Acts 28. 17–end ct		G	Ecclus. 21. 1–17 or Ezek. 24. 15–end Mark 16. 9–end	2 Kings 17. 1–23 Acts 28. 17–end ct

October 2011

			Sunday Principal Service Weekday Eucharist	Third Service Morning Prayer
30	S	THE FOURTH SUNDAY BEFORE ADVENT	Mic. 3. 5–end Ps. 43 or Ps. 107. 1–8 1 Thess. 2. 9–13	Ps. 33 Isa. 66. 20–23 Eph. 1. 11–end
	G		Matt. 24. 1–14	
	⑳	or ALL SAINTS' SUNDAY (see readings for 1 November throughout the day)		
31 DEL 31	M	Martin Luther, Reformer, 1546	Rom. 11. 29–end Ps. 69. 31–37 Luke 14. 12–14	Ps. 2; 146 alt. Ps. 98; 99; 101 Isa. 1. 1–20 Matt. 1. 18–end
	G*			

November 2011

1	Tu	**ALL SAINTS' DAY**		Rev. 7. 9–17 Ps. 34. 1–10 1 John 3. 1–3	MP: Ps. 15; 84; 149 Isa. ch. 35 Luke 9. 18–27
	⑳			Matt. 5. 1–12	
		or, if the readings above are used on Sunday 30 October:		Isa. 56. 3–8 or 2 Esdras 2. 42–end Ps. 33. 1–5 Heb. 12. 18–24	MP: Ps. 111; 112; 117 Wisd. 5. 1–16 or Jer. 31. 31–34 2 Cor. 4. 5–12
	⑳			Matt. 5. 1–12	
		or, if kept as a feria:		Rom. 12. 5–16 Ps. 131 Luke 14. 15–24	Ps. 5; 147. 1–12 alt. Ps. 106† (or 103) Isa. 1. 21–end Matt. 2. 1–15
	R or G				
2	W	**Commemoration of the Faithful Departed (All Souls' Day)**			
		Lam. 3. 17–26, 31–33 or Wisd. 3. 1–9 Ps. 23 or Ps. 27. 1–6, 16–end Rom. 5. 5–11 or 1 Pet. 1. 3–9 John 5. 19–25 or John 6. 37–40	or	Rom. 13. 8–10 Ps. 112 Luke 14. 25–33	Ps. 9; 147. 13–end alt. Ps. 110; 111; 112 Isa. 2. 1–11 Matt. 2. 16–end
	Rp or Gp				
3	Th	**Richard Hooker, Priest, Anglican Apologist, Teacher, 1600** Martin of Porres, Friar, 1639			
		Com. Teacher esp. John 16. 12–15 also Ecclus. 44. 10–15	or	Rom. 14. 7–12 Ps. 27. 14–end Luke 15. 1–10	Ps. 11; 15; 148 alt. Ps. 113; 115 Isa. 2. 12–end Matt. ch. 3
	Rw or Gw				
4	F			Rom. 15. 14–21 Ps. 98 Luke 16. 1–8	Ps. 16; 149 alt. Ps. 139 Isa. 3. 1–15 Matt. 4. 1–11
	R or G				

*R or G if All Saints is celebrated on 30 October.

Second Service Evening Prayer		Calendar and Holy Communion	Morning Prayer	Evening Prayer
Ps. 111; 117 Dan. 7. 1–18 Luke 6. 17–31		**THE NINETEENTH SUNDAY AFTER TRINITY** Gen. 18. 23–32 Ps. 141. 1–9 Eph. 4. 17–end Matt. 9. 1–8	Ps. 33 Isa. 66. 20–23 Eph. 1. 11–end	Ps. 111; 117 Dan. 7. 1–18 Luke 6. 17–31
	G			
First EP of All Saints Ps. 1; 5 Ecclus. 44. 1–15 *or* Isa. 40. 27–end Rev. 19. 6–10 ℣ **ct** *or, if All Saints is observed on 30 October:* Ps. **92**; 96; 97 *alt.* Ps. **105**† (*or* 103) Dan. ch. 1 Rev. ch. 1			Isa. 1. 1–20 Matt. 1. 18–end	*First EP of All Saints* Ps. 1; 5 Ecclus. 44. 1–15 *or* Isa. 40. 27–end Rev. 19. 6–10
	G			℣ **ct**
EP: Ps. 148; 150 Isa. 65. 17–end Heb. 11.32 – 12.2		**ALL SAINTS' DAY** Isa. 66. 20–23 Ps. 33. 1–5 Rev. 7. 2–4 [5–8] 9–12 Matt. 5. 1–12	Ps. 15; 84; 149 Isa. ch. 35 Luke 9. 18–27	Ps. 148; 150 Isa. 65. 17–end Heb. 11.32 – 12.2
EP: Ps. 145 Isa. 66. 20–23 Col. 1. 9–14				
Ps. 98; 99; **100** *alt.* Ps. 107† Dan. 2. 1–24 Rev. 2. 1–11	℣			
Ps. 111; **112**; 116 *alt.* Ps. 119. 129–152 Dan. 2. 25–end Rev. 2. 12–end		To celebrate All Souls' Day, see *Common Worship* provision. Isa. 2. 1–11 Matt. 2. 16–end		Dan. 2. 25–end Rev. 2. 12–end
	G			
Ps. 118 *alt.* Ps. 114; **116**; 117 Dan. 3. 1–18 Rev. 3. 1–13			Isa. 2. 12–end Matt. ch. 3	Dan. 3. 1–18 Rev. 3. 1–13
	G			
Ps. 137; 138; **143** *alt.* Ps. **130**; 131; 137 Dan. 3. 19–end Rev. 3. 14–end			Isa. 3. 1–15 Matt. 4. 1–11	Dan. 3. 19–end Rev. 3. 14–end
	G			

November 2011

			Sunday Principal Service Weekday Eucharist	Third Service Morning Prayer
5 R or G	Sa		Rom. 16. 3–9, 16, 22–end Ps. 145. 1–7 Luke 16. 9–15	Ps. *18. 31–end*; 150 *alt.* Ps. 120; *121*; 122 Isa. 4.2 – 5.7 Matt. 4. 12–22
6 R or G	S	**THE THIRD SUNDAY BEFORE ADVENT** Wisd. 6. 12–16 *or* *Canticle:* Wisd. 6. 17–20 1 Thess. 4. 13–end Matt. 25. 1–13	Amos 5. 18–24 Ps. 70 1 Thess. 4. 13–end Matt. 25. 1–13	Ps. 91 Deut. 17. 14–end 1 Tim. 2. 1–7
7 DEL 32 Rw or Gw	M	**Willibrord of York, Bishop, Apostle of Frisia, 739** Com. Missionary *or* *esp.* Isa. 52. 7–10 Matt. 28. 16–end	Wisd. 1. 1–7 *or* Titus 1. 1–9 Ps. 139. 1–9 *or* Ps. 24. 1–6 Luke 17. 1–6	Ps. 19; *20* *alt.* Ps. 123; 124; 125; *126* Isa. 5. 8–24 Matt. 4.23 – 5.12
8 Rw or Gw	Tu	**The Saints and Martyrs of England** Isa. 61. 4–9 *or* *or* Ecclus. 44. 1–15 Ps. 15 Rev. 19. 5–10 John 17. 18–23	Wisd. 2.23 – 3.9 *or* Titus 2. 1–8, 11–14 Ps. 34. 1–6 *or* Ps. 37. 3–5, 30–32 Luke 17. 7–10	Ps. *21*; 24 *alt.* Ps. *132*; 133 Isa. 5. 25–end Matt. 5. 13–20
9 R or G	W	*Margery Kempe, Mystic, c. 1440*	Wisd. 6. 1–11 *or* Titus 3. 1–7 Ps. 82 *or* Ps. 23 Luke 17. 11–19	Ps. *23*; 25 *alt.* Ps. 119. 153–end Isa. ch. 6 Matt. 5. 21–37
10 Rw or Gw	Th	**Leo the Great, Bishop of Rome, Teacher, 461** Com. Teacher *or* *also* 1 Pet. 5. 1–11	Wisd. 7.22 – 8.1 *or* Philemon 7–20 Ps. 119. 89–96 *or* Ps. 146. 4–end Luke 17. 20–25	Ps. *26*; 27 *alt.* Ps. *143*; 146 Isa. 7. 1–17 Matt. 5. 38–end
11 Rw or Gw	F	**Martin, Bishop of Tours, c. 397** Com. Bishop *or* *also* 1 Thess. 5. 1–11 Matt. 25. 34–40	Wisd. 13. 1–9 *or* 2 John 4–9 Ps. 19. 1–4 *or* Ps. 119. 1–8 Luke 17. 26–end	Ps. 28; *32* *alt.* Ps. 142; *144* Isa. 8. 1–15 Matt. 6. 1–18
12 R or G	Sa		Wisd. 18. 14–16; 19. 6–9 *or* 3 John 5–8 Ps. 105. 1–5, 35–42 *or* Ps. 112 Luke 18. 1–8	Ps. 33 *alt.* Ps. 147 Isa. 8.16 – 9.7 Matt. 6. 19–end
13 R or G	S	**THE SECOND SUNDAY BEFORE ADVENT** (Remembrance Sunday)	Zeph. 1. 7, 12–end Ps. 90. 1–8 [9–11] 12 (*or* 90. 1–8) 1 Thess. 5. 1–11 Matt. 25. 14–30	Ps. 98 Dan. 10. 19–end Rev. ch. 4

Second Service Evening Prayer		Calendar and Holy Communion	Morning Prayer	Evening Prayer
Ps. 145 alt. Ps. 118 Dan. 4. 1–18 Rev. ch. 4 ct	G		Isa. 4.2 – 5.7 Matt. 4. 12–22	Dan. 4. 1–18 Rev. ch. 4 ct
Ps. [20]; 82 Judges 7. 2–22 John 15. 9–17	G	**THE TWENTIETH SUNDAY AFTER TRINITY** Prov. 9. 1–6 Ps. 145. 15–end Eph. 5. 15–21 Matt. 22. 1–14	Ps. 91 Deut. 17. 14–end 1 Tim. 2. 1–7	Ps. [20]; 82 Judges 7. 2–22 John 15. 9–17
Ps. 34 alt. Ps. 127; 128; 129 Dan. 4. 19–end Rev. ch. 5	G		Isa. 5. 8–24 Matt. 4.23 – 5.12	Dan. 4. 19–end Rev. ch. 5
Ps. 36; 40 alt. Ps. (134); 135 Dan. 5. 1–12 Rev. ch. 6	G		Isa. 5. 25–end Matt. 5. 13–20	Dan. 5. 1–12 Rev. ch. 6
Ps. 37 alt. Ps. 136 Dan. 5. 13–end Rev. 7. 1–4, 9–end	G		Isa. ch. 6 Matt. 5. 21–37	Dan. 5. 13–end Rev. 7. 1–4, 9–end
Ps. 42; 43 alt. Ps. 138; 140; 141 Dan. ch. 6 Rev. ch. 8	G		Isa. 7. 1–17 Matt. 5. 38–end	Dan. ch. 6 Rev. ch. 8
Ps. 31 alt. Ps. 145 Dan. 7. 1–14 Rev. 9. 1–12	Gw	**Martin, Bishop of Tours, c. 397** Com. Bishop	Isa. 8. 1–15 Matt. 6. 1–18	Dan. 7. 1–14 Rev. 9. 1–12
Ps. 84; 86 alt. Ps. 148; 149; 150 Dan. 7. 15–end Rev. 9. 13–end ct	G		Isa. 8.16 – 9.7 Matt. 6. 19–end	Dan. 7. 15–end Rev. 9. 13–end ct
Ps. 89. 19–37 (or 89. 19–29) 1 Kings 1. [1–14] 15–40 Rev. 1. 4–18 Gospel: Luke 9. 1–6	G	**THE TWENTY-FIRST SUNDAY AFTER TRINITY** Gen. 32. 24–29 Ps. 90. 1–12 Eph. 6. 10–20 John 4. 46b–end	Ps. 98 Dan. 10. 19–end Rev. ch. 4	Ps. 89. 19–37 (or 89. 19–29) 1 Kings 1. [1–14] 15–40 Rev. 1. 4–18

November 2011

		Sunday Principal Service / Weekday Eucharist	Third Service / Morning Prayer

14
DEL 33

M — Samuel Seabury, first Anglican Bishop in North America, 1796

1 Macc. 1. 10–15, 41–43, 54–57, 62–64
or Rev. 1. 1–4; 2. 1–5
Ps. 79. 1–5
or Ps. 1

Ps. 46; **47**
alt. Ps. 1; 2; 3
Isa. 9.8 – 10.4
Matt. 7. 1–12

R or G — Luke 18. 35–end

15

Tu

2 Macc. 6. 18–end
or Rev. 3. 1–6, 14–31
Ps. 11
or Ps. 15

Ps. 48; **52**
alt. Ps. **5**; 6; (8)
Isa. 10. 5–19
Matt. 7. 13–end

R or G — Luke 19. 1–10

16

W — **Margaret, Queen of Scotland, Philanthropist, Reformer of the Church, 1093**
Edmund Rich of Abingdon, Archbishop of Canterbury, 1240

Com. Saint   or
also Prov. 31. 10–12, 20, 26–end
1 Cor. 12.13 – 13.3
Matt. 25. 34–end

2 Macc. 7. 1, 20–31
or Rev. ch. 4
Ps. 116. 10–end
or Ps. 150
Luke 19. 11–28

Ps. **56**; 57
alt. Ps. 119. 1–32
Isa. 10. 20–32
Matt. 8. 1–13

Rw or Gw

17

Th — **Hugh, Bishop of Lincoln, 1200**
Com. Bishop   or
also 1 Tim. 6. 11–16

1 Macc. 2. 15–29
or Rev. 5. 1–10
Ps. 129
or Ps. 149. 1–5
Luke 19. 41–44

Ps. 61; **62**
alt. Ps. 14; **15**; 16
Isa. 10.33 – 11.9
Matt. 8. 14–22

Rw or Gw

18

F — **Elizabeth of Hungary, Princess of Thuringia, Philanthropist, 1231**
Com. Saint   or
esp. Matt. 25. 31–end
also Prov. 31. 10–end

1 Macc. 4. 36–37, 52–59
or Rev. 10. 8–11
Ps. 122
or Ps. 119. 65–72
Luke 19. 45–48

Ps. **63**; 65
alt. Ps. 17; **19**
Isa. 11.10 – 12.end
Matt. 8. 23–end

Rw or Gw

19

Sa — **Hilda, Abbess of Whitby, 680**
Mechtild, Béguine of Magdeburg, Mystic, 1280
Com. Religious   or
esp. Isa. 61.10 – 62.5

1 Macc. 6. 1–13
or Rev. 11. 4–12
Ps. 124
or Ps. 144. 1–9
Luke 20. 27–40

Ps. 78. 1–39
alt. Ps. 20; 21; **23**
Isa. 13. 1–13
Matt. 9. 1–17

Rw or Gw

20

S — **CHRIST THE KING**
The Sunday Next Before Advent

Ezek. 34. 11–16, 20–24
Ps. 95. 1–7
Eph. 1. 15–end
Matt. 25. 31–end

MP: Ps. 29; 110
Isa. 4.2 – 5.7
Luke 19. 29–38

R or W

21
DEL 34

M

Dan. 1. 1–6, 8–20
Canticle: Bless the Lord
Luke 21. 1–4

Ps. 92; 96
alt. Ps. 27; **30**
Isa. 14. 3–20
Matt. 9. 18–34

R or G

22

Tu — *Cecilia, Martyr at Rome, c. 230*

Dan. 2. 31–45
Canticle: Benedicite 1–3
Luke 21. 5–11

Ps. **97**; 98; 100
alt. Ps. 32; **36**
Isa. ch. 17
Matt. 9.35 – 10.15

R or G

Second Service Evening Prayer		Calendar and Holy Communion	Morning Prayer	Evening Prayer
Ps. 70; *71* *alt.* Ps. *4*; 7 Dan. 8. 1–14 Rev. ch. 10	G		Isa. 9.8 – 10.4 Matt. 7. 1–12	Dan. 8. 1–14 Rev. ch. 10
Ps. *67*; 72 *alt.* Ps. *9*; 10† Dan. 8. 15–end Rev. 11. 1–14	Gw	**Machutus, Bishop, Apostle of Brittany, c. 564** Com. Bishop	Isa. 10. 5–19 Matt. 7. 13–end	Dan. 8. 15–end Rev. 11. 1–14
Ps. 73 *alt.* Ps. *11*; 12; 13 Dan. 9. 1–19 Rev. 11. 15–end	G		Isa. 10. 20–32 Matt. 8. 1–13	Dan. 9. 1–19 Rev. 11. 15–end
Ps. 74; *76* *alt.* Ps. 18† Dan. 9. 20–end Rev. ch. 12	Gw	**Hugh, Bishop of Lincoln, 1200** Com. Bishop	Isa. 10.33 – 11.9 Matt. 8. 14–22	Dan. 9. 20–end Rev. ch. 12
Ps. 77 *alt.* Ps. 22 Dan. 10.1 – 11.1 Rev. 13. 1–10	G		Isa. 11.10 – 12.end Matt. 8. 23–end	Dan. 10.1 – 11.1 Rev. 13. 1–10
Ps. 78. 40–end *alt.* Ps. *24*; 25 Dan. ch. 12 Rev. 13. 11–end **ct** *or First EP of Christ the King* Ps. 99; 100 Isa. 10.33 – 11.9 1 Tim. 6. 11–16 **R** *or* **W ct**	G		Isa. 13. 1–13 Matt. 9. 1–17	Dan. ch. 12 Rev. 13. 11–end **ct**
EP: Ps. 93; [97] 2 Sam. 23. 1–7 *or* 1 Macc. 2. 15–29 Matt. 28. 16–end	G	**THE SUNDAY NEXT BEFORE ADVENT** To celebrate Christ the King, see *Common Worship* provision. Jer. 23. 5–8 Ps. 85. 8–end Col. 1. 13–20 John 6. 5–14	Ps. 29; 110 Isa. 4.2 – 5.7 Luke 19. 29–38	Ps. 93; [97] 2 Sam. 23. 1–7 *or* 1 Macc. 2. 15–29 Matt. 28. 16–end
Ps. *80*; 81 *alt.* Ps. 26; *28*; 29 Isa. 40. 1–11 Rev. 14. 1–13	G		Isa. 14. 3–20 Matt. 9. 18–34	Isa. 40. 1–11 Rev. 14. 1–13
Ps. 99; *101* *alt.* Ps. 33 Isa. 40. 12–26 Rev. 14.14 – 15.end	Gr	**Cecilia, Martyr at Rome, c. 230** Com. Virgin Martyr	Isa. ch. 17 Matt. 9.35 – 10.15	Isa. 40. 12–26 Rev. 14.14 – 15.end

November 2011

			Sunday Principal Service Weekday Eucharist	Third Service Morning Prayer
23	W	**Clement, Bishop of Rome, Martyr, c. 100** Com. Martyr or *also* Phil. 3.17 – 4.3 Matt. 16. 13–19	Dan. 5. 1–6, 13–14, 16–17, 23–28 *Canticle*: Benedicite 4–5 Luke 21. 12–19	Ps. 110; 111; *112* *alt.* Ps. 34 Isa. ch. 19 Matt. 10. 16–33
	R *or* Gr			
24	Th		Dan. 6. 12–end *Canticle*: Benedicite 6–8a Luke 21. 20–28	Ps. *125*; 126; 127; 128 *alt.* Ps. 37† Isa. 21. 1–12 Matt. 10.34 – 11.1
	R *or* G			
25	F	*Catherine of Alexandria, Martyr, 4th century; Isaac Watts, Hymn Writer, 1748* Dan. 7. 2–14 *Canticle*: Benedicite 8b–10a Luke 21. 29–33		Ps. 139 *alt.* Ps. 31 Isa. 22. 1–14 Matt. 11. 2–19
	R *or* G			
26	Sa		Dan. 7. 15–27 *Canticle*: Benedicite 10b–end Luke 21. 34–36	Ps. 145 *alt.* Ps. 41; *42*; 43 Isa. ch. 24 Matt. 11. 20–end
	R *or* G			
27	S	**THE FIRST SUNDAY OF ADVENT** CW Year B begins	Isa. 64. 1–9 Ps. 80. 1–8, 18–20 (*or* 80. 1–8) 1 Cor. 1. 3–9 Mark 13. 24–end	Ps. 44 Isa. 2. 1–5 Luke 12. 35–48
	P			
28	M	Daily Eucharistic Lectionary Year 2 begins	Isa. 2. 1–5 Ps. 122 Matt. 8. 5–11	Ps. *50*; 54 *alt.* Ps. *1*; 2; 3 Isa. 25. 1–9 Matt. 12. 1–21
	P			
29	Tu		Isa. 11. 1–10 Ps. 72. 1–4, 18–19 Luke 10. 21–24	Ps. *80*; 82 *alt.* Ps. *5*; 6; (8) Isa. 26. 1–13 Matt. 12. 22–37
		Day of Intercession and Thanksgiving for the Missionary Work of the Church	Isa. 49. 1–6; Isa. 52. 7–10; Mic. 4. 1–5 Ps. 2; 46; 47 Acts 17. 12–end; 2 Cor. 5.14 – 6.2; Eph. 2. 13–end Matt. 5. 13–16; Matt. 28. 16–end; John 17. 20–end	
	P			
30	W	**ANDREW THE APOSTLE**	Isa. 52. 7–10 Ps. 19. 1–6 Rom. 10. 12–18 Matt. 4. 18–22	MP: Ps. 47; 147. 1–12 Ezek. 47. 1–12 *or* Ecclus. 14. 20–end John 12. 20–32
	R			

December 2011

1	Th	*Charles de Foucauld, Hermit in the Sahara, 1916* Isa. 26. 1–6 Ps. 118. 18–27a Matt. 7. 21, 24–27		Ps. *42*; 43 *alt.* Ps. 14; *15*; 16 Isa. 28. 14–end Matt. 13. 1–23
	P			

Second Service Evening Prayer		Calendar and Holy Communion	Morning Prayer	Evening Prayer
		Clement, Bishop of Rome, Martyr, c. 100		
Ps. 121; *122*; 123; 124 alt. Ps. 119. 33–56 Isa. 40.27 – 41.7 Rev. 16. 1–11	Gr	Com. Martyr	Isa. ch. 19 Matt. 10. 16–33	Isa. 40.27 – 41.7 Rev. 16. 1–11
Ps. 131; 132; *133* alt. Ps. 39; *40* Isa. 41. 8–20 Rev. 16. 12–end	G		Isa. 21. 1–12 Matt. 10.34 – 11.1	Isa. 41. 8–20 Rev. 16. 12–end
		Catherine of Alexandria, Martyr, 4th century		
Ps. *146*; 147 alt. Ps. 35 Isa. 41.21 – 42.9 Rev. ch. 17	Gr	Com. Virgin Martyr	Isa. 22. 1–14 Matt. 11. 2–19	Isa. 41.21 – 42.9 Rev. ch. 17
Ps. 148; 149; *150* alt. Ps. 45; *46* Isa. 42. 10–17 Rev. ch. 18 **P ct**	G		Isa. ch. 24 Matt. 11. 20–end	Isa. 42. 10–17 Rev. ch. 18 **P ct**
		THE FIRST SUNDAY OF ADVENT		
Ps. 25 (*or* 25. 1–9) Isa. 1. 1–20 Matt. 21. 1–13	P	Advent 1 Collect until Christmas Eve Mic. 4. 1–4, 6–7 Ps. 25. 1–9 Rom. 13. 8–14 Matt. 21. 1–13	Ps. 44 Isa. 2. 1–5 Luke 12. 35–48	Ps. 9 Isa. 1. 1–20 Mark 13. 24–37
Ps. 70; *71* alt. Ps. *4*; 7 Isa. 42. 18–end Rev. ch. 19	P		Isa. 25. 1–9 Matt. 12. 1–21	Isa. 42. 18–end Rev. ch. 19
Ps. *74*; 75 alt. Ps. *9*; 10† Isa. 43. 1–13 Rev. ch. 20 *or First EP of Andrew the Apostle* Ps. 48 Isa. 49. 1–9a 1 Cor. 4. 9–16 **R ct**			Isa. 26. 1–13 Matt. 12. 22–37	Isa. 43. 1–13 Rev. ch. 20 *or First EP of Andrew the Apostle* (Ps. 48) Isa. 49. 1–9a 1 Cor. 4. 9–16
		To celebrate the Day of Intercession and Thanksgiving for the Missionary Work of the Church, see *Common Worship* provision.		
	P			**R ct**
EP: Ps. 87; 96 Zech. 8. 20–end John 1. 35–42	R	ANDREW THE APOSTLE Zech. 8. 20–end Ps. 92. 1–5 Rom. 10. 9–end Matt. 4. 18–22	(Ps. 47; 147. 1–12) Ezek. 47. 1–12 *or* Ecclus. 14. 20–end John 12. 20–32	(Ps. 87; 96) Isa. 52. 7–10 John 1. 35–42
Ps. *40*; 46 alt. Ps. 18† Isa. 44. 1–8 Rev. 21. 9–21	P		Isa. 28. 14–end Matt. 13. 1–23	Isa. 44. 1–8 Rev. 21. 9–21

December 2011

		Sunday Principal Service Weekday Eucharist	Third Service Morning Prayer
2	F	Isa. 29. 17–end Ps. 27. 1–4, 16–17 Matt. 9. 27–31	Ps. *25*; 26 *alt.* Ps. 17; *19* Isa. 29. 1–14
	P		Matt. 13. 24–43
3	Sa	*Francis Xavier, Missionary, Apostle of the Indies, 1552* Isa. 30. 19–21, 23–26 Ps. 146. 4–9 Matt. 9.35 – 10.1, 6–8	Ps. *9*; (10) *alt.* Ps. 20; 21; *23* Isa. 29. 15–end
	P		Matt. 13. 44–end
4	S	THE SECOND SUNDAY OF ADVENT	
		Isa. 40. 1–11 Ps. 85. 1–2, 8–end (*or* 85. 8–end) 2 Pet. 3. 8–15a	Ps. 80 Baruch 5. 1–9 *or* Zeph. 3. 14–end Luke 1. 5–20
	P	Mark 1. 1–8	
5	M	Isa. ch. 35 Ps. 85. 7–end Luke 5. 17–26	Ps. 44 *alt.* Ps. 27; *30* Isa. 30. 1–18
	P		Matt. 14. 1–12
6	Tu	**Nicholas, Bishop of Myra, c. 326** Com. Bishop *or* *also* Isa. 61. 1–3 1 Tim. 6. 6–11	Isa. 40. 1–11 Ps. 96. 1, 10–end Matt. 18. 12–14	Ps. *56*; 57 *alt.* Ps. 32; *36* Isa. 30. 19–end
	Pw	Mark 10. 13–16		Matt. 14. 13–end
7	W	**Ambrose, Bishop of Milan, Teacher, 397** Ember Day* Com. Teacher *or* *also* Isa. 41. 9b–13 Luke 22. 24–30	Isa. 40. 25–end Ps. 103. 8–13 Matt. 11. 28–end	Ps. *62*; 63 *alt.* Ps. 34 Isa. ch. 31
	Pw			Matt. 15. 1–20
8	Th	**The Conception of the Blessed Virgin Mary** Com. BVM *or*	Isa. 41. 13–20 Ps. 145. 1, 8–13 Matt. 11. 11–15	Ps. 53; *54*; 60 *alt.* Ps. 37† Isa. ch. 32
	Pw			Matt. 15. 21–28
9	F	Ember Day*		
			Isa. 48. 17–19 Ps. 1 Matt. 11. 16–19	Ps. 85; *86* *alt.* Ps. 31 Isa. 33. 1–22
	P			Matt. 15. 29–end
10	Sa	Ember Day*		
			Ecclus. 48. 1–4, 9–11 *or* 2 Kings 2. 9–12 Ps. 80. 1–4, 18–19 Matt. 17. 10–13	Ps. 145 *alt.* Ps. 41; *42*; 43 Isa. ch. 35
	P			Matt. 16. 1–12
11	S	THE THIRD SUNDAY OF ADVENT		
			Isa. 61. 1–4, 8–end Ps. 126 *or Canticle*: Magnificat 1 Thess. 5. 16–24	Ps. 50. 1–6, 62 Isa. ch. 12 Luke 1. 57–66
	P		John 1. 6–8, 19–28	
12	M	Num. 24. 2–7, 15–17 Ps. 25. 3–8 Matt. 21. 23–27	Ps. 40 *alt.* Ps. 44 Isa. 38. 1–8, 21–22
	P			Matt. 16. 13–end

*For Ember Day provision, see p. 13.

Second Service Evening Prayer	Calendar and Holy Communion	Morning Prayer	Evening Prayer
Ps. 16; *17* *alt*. Ps. 22 Isa. 44. 9–23 Rev. 21.22 – 22.5	P	Isa. 29. 1–14 Matt. 13. 24–43	Isa. 44. 9–23 Rev. 21.22 – 22.5
Ps. *27*; 28 *alt*. Ps. *24*; 25 Isa. 44.24 – 45.13 Rev. 22. 6–end ct	P	Isa. 29. 15–end Matt. 13. 44–end	Isa. 44.24 – 45.13 Rev. 22. 6–end ct
Ps. 40 (*or* 40. 12–end) 1 Kings 22. 1–28 Rom. 15. 4–13 *Gospel*: Matt. 11. 2–11	**THE SECOND SUNDAY OF ADVENT** 2 Kings 22. 8–10; 23. 1–3 Ps. 50. 1–6 Rom. 15. 4–13 Luke 21. 25–33 P	Ps. 80 Baruch 5. 1–9 *or* Zeph. 3. 14–end Luke 1. 5–20	Ps. 40 (*or* 40. 12–end) 1 Kings 22. 1–28 2 Pet. 3. 8–15a
Ps. *144*; 146 *alt*. Ps. 26; *28*; 29 Isa. 45. 14–end 1 Thess. ch. 1	P	Isa. 30. 1–18 Matt. 14. 1–12	Isa. 45. 14–end 1 Thess. ch. 1
Ps. *11*; 12; 13 *alt*. Ps. 33 Isa. ch. 46 1 Thess. 2. 1–12	**Nicholas, Bishop of Myra, c. 326** Com. Bishop Pw	Isa. 30. 19–end Matt. 14. 13–end	Isa. ch. 46 1 Thess. 2. 1–12
Ps. *10*; 14 *alt*. Ps. 119. 33–56 Isa. ch. 47 1 Thess. 2. 13–end	P	Isa. ch. 31 Matt. 15. 1–20	Isa. ch. 47 1 Thess. 2. 13–end
Ps. 73 *alt*. Ps. 39; *40* Isa. 48. 1–11 1 Thess. ch. 3	**The Conception of the Blessed Virgin Mary** Isa. ch. 32 Matt. 15. 21–28 Pw	Isa. ch. 32 Matt. 15. 21–28	Isa. 48. 1–11 1 Thess. ch. 3
Ps. 82; *90* *alt*. Ps. 35 Isa. 48. 12–end 1 Thess. 4. 1–12	P	Isa. 33. 1–22 Matt. 15. 29–end	Isa. 48. 12–end 1 Thess. 4. 1–12
Ps. 93; *94* *alt*. Ps. 45; *46* Isa. 49. 1–13 1 Thess. 4. 13–end ct	P	Isa. ch. 35 Matt. 16. 1–12	Isa. 49. 1–13 1 Thess. 4. 13–end ct
Ps. 68. 1–19 (*or* 68. 1–8) Mal. 3. 1–4; ch. 4 Phil. 4. 4–7 *Gospel*: Matt. 14. 1–12	**THE THIRD SUNDAY OF ADVENT** Isa. ch. 35 Ps. 80. 1–7 1 Cor. 4. 1–5 Matt. 11. 2–10 P	Ps. 62 Isa. ch. 12 Luke 1. 57–66	Ps. 68. 1–19 (*or* 68. 1–8) Mal. 3. 1–4; ch. 4 Matt. 14. 1–12
Ps. 25; *26* *alt*. Ps. *47*; 49 Isa. 49. 14–25 1 Thess. 5. 1–11	P	Isa. 38. 1–8, 21–22 Matt. 16. 13–end	Isa. 49. 14–25 1 Thess. 5. 1–11

December 2011

			Sunday Principal Service Weekday Eucharist	Third Service Morning Prayer
13	Tu Pr	**Lucy, Martyr at Syracuse, 304** *Samuel Johnson, Moralist, 1784* Com. Martyr *also* Wisd. 3. 1–7 2 Cor. 4. 6–15	*or*	Zeph. 3. 1–2, 9–13 Ps. 34. 1–6, 21–22 Matt. 21. 28–32	Ps. **70**; 74 *alt.* Ps. **48**; 52 Isa. 38. 9–20 Matt. 17. 1–13
14	W Pw	**John of the Cross, Poet, Teacher, 1591** Com. Teacher *esp.* 1 Cor. 2. 1–10 *also* John 14. 18–23	*or*	Isa. 45. 6b–8, 18, 21b–end Ps. 85. 7–end Luke 7. 18b–23	Ps. **75**; 96 *alt.* Ps. 119. 57–80 Isa. ch. 39 Matt. 17. 14–21
15	Th P			Isa. 54. 1–10 Ps. 30. 1–5, 11–end Luke 7. 24–30	Ps. **76**; 97 *alt.* Ps. 56; **57**; (63†) Zeph. 1.1 – 2.3 Matt. 17. 22–end
16	F P			Isa. 56. 1–3a, 6–8 Ps. 67 John 5. 33–36	Ps. 77; **98** *alt.* Ps. **51**; 54 Zeph. 3. 1–13 Matt. 18. 1–20
17	Sa P	O Sapientia *Eglantyne Jebb, Social Reformer, Founder of 'Save the Children', 1928*		Gen. 49. 2, 8–10 Ps. 72. 1–5, 18–19 Matt. 1. 1–17	Ps. 71 *alt.* Ps. 68 Zeph. 3. 14–end Matt. 18. 21–end
18	S P	THE FOURTH SUNDAY OF ADVENT		2 Sam. 7. 1–11, 16 *Canticle:* Magnificat *or* Ps. 89. 1–4, 19–26 (*or* 1–8) Rom. 16. 25–end Luke 1. 26–38	Ps. 144 Isa. 7. 10–16 Rom. 1. 1–7
19	M P			Judg. 13. 2–7, 24–end Ps. 71. 3–8 Luke 1. 5–25	Ps. 144; **146** Mal. 1. 1, 6–end Matt. 19. 1–12
20	Tu P			Isa. 7. 10–14 Ps. 24. 1–6 Luke 1. 26–38	Ps. **46**; 95 Mal. 2. 1–16 Matt. 19. 13–15
21	W* P			Zeph. 3. 14–18 Ps. 33. 1–4, 11–12, 20–end Luke 1. 39–45	Ps. **121**; 122; 123 Mal. 2.17 – 3.12 Matt. 19. 16–end
22	Th P			1 Sam. 1. 24–end Ps. 113 Luke 1. 46–56	Ps. **124**; 125; 126; 127 Mal. 3.13 – 4.end Matt. 23. 1–12
23	F P			Mal. 3. 1–4; 4. 5–end Ps. 25. 3–9 Luke 1. 57–66	Ps. 128; 129; **130**; 131 Nahum ch. 1 Matt. 23. 13–28
24	Sa P	CHRISTMAS EVE		*Morning Eucharist* 2 Sam. 7. 1–5, 8–11, 16 Ps. 89. 2, 19–27 Acts 13. 16–26 Luke 1. 67–79	Ps. **45**; 113 Obadiah Matt. 23. 29–end

*Thomas the Apostle may be celebrated on 21 December instead of 3 July.

Second Service Evening Prayer	Calendar and Holy Communion	Morning Prayer	Evening Prayer
	Lucy, Martyr at Syracuse, 304 Com. Virgin Martyr		
Ps. *50*; 54 *alt.* Ps. 50 Isa. ch. 50 1 Thess. 5. 12–end **Pr**		Isa. 38. 9–20 Matt. 17. 1–13	Isa. ch. 50 1 Thess. 5. 12–end
Ps. 25; *82* *alt.* Ps. *59*; 60; (67) Isa. 51. 1–8 2 Thess. ch. 1 **P**	Ember Day Ember CEG	Isa. ch. 39 Matt. 17. 14–21	Isa. 51. 1–8 2 Thess. ch. 1
Ps. 44 *alt.* Ps. 61; *62*; 64 Isa. 51. 9–16 2 Thess. ch. 2 **P**		Zeph. 1.1 – 2.3 Matt. 17. 22–end	Isa. 51. 9–16 2 Thess. ch. 2
Ps. 49 *alt.* Ps. 38 Isa. 51. 17–end 2 Thess. ch. 3 **P**	O Sapientia Ember Day Ember CEG	Zeph. 3. 1–13 Matt. 18. 1–20	Isa. 51. 17–end 2 Thess. ch. 3
Ps. 42; *43* *alt.* Ps. 65; *66* Isa. 52. 1–12 Jude **ct** **P**	Ember Day Ember CEG	Zeph. 3. 14–end Matt. 18. 21–end	Isa. 52. 1–12 Jude **ct**
Ps. 113; [131] Zech. 2. 10–end Luke 1. 39–55 **P**	**THE FOURTH SUNDAY OF ADVENT** Isa. 40. 1–9 Ps. 145. 17–end Phil. 4. 4–7 John 1. 19–28	Ps. 144 Isa. 7. 10–16 Rom. 1. 1–7	Ps. 113; [131] Zech. 2. 10–end Luke 1. 39–55
Ps. 10; *57* Isa. 52.13 – 53.end 2 Pet. 1. 1–15 **P**		Mal. 1. 1, 6–end Matt. 19. 1–12	Isa. 52.13 – 53.end 2 Pet. 1. 1–15
Ps. *4*; 9 Isa. ch. 54 2 Pet. 1.16 – 2.3 **P**		Mal. 2. 1–16 Matt. 19. 13–15	Isa. ch. 54 2 Pet. 1.16 – 2.3 *or First EP of Thomas* (Ps. 27) Isa. ch. 35 Heb. 10.35 – 11.1 **R ct**
Ps. 80; *84* Isa. ch. 55 2 Pet. 2. 4–end **R**	**THOMAS THE APOSTLE** Job 42. 1–6 Ps. 139. 1–11 Eph. 2. 19–end John 20. 24–end	(Ps. 92; 146) 2 Sam. 15. 17–21 *or* Ecclus. ch. 2 John 11. 1–16	(Ps. 139) Hab. 2. 1–4 1 Pet. 1. 3–12
Ps. 24; *48* Isa. 56. 1–8 2 Pet. ch. 3 **P**		Mal. 3.13 – 4.end Matt. 23. 1–12	Isa. ch. 56. 1–8 2 Pet. ch. 3
Ps. 89. 1–37 Isa. 63. 1–6 2 John **P**		Nahum ch. 1 Matt. 23. 13–28	Isa. 63. 1–6 2 John
Ps. 85 Zech. ch. 2 Rev. 1. 1–8 **P**	**CHRISTMAS EVE** Coll. (1) Christmas Eve (2) Advent 1 Mic. 5. 2–5a Ps. 24 Titus 3. 3–7 Luke 2. 1–14	Obadiah Matt. 23. 29–end	Zech. ch. 2 Rev. 1. 1–8

December 2011

			Sunday Principal Service Weekday Eucharist	Third Service Morning Prayer
25	S	**CHRISTMAS DAY** *Any of the following sets of readings may be used on the evening of Christmas Eve and on Christmas Day. Set III should be used at some service during the celebration.*	*I* Isa. 9. 2–7 Ps. 96 Titus 2. 11–14 Luke 2. 1–14 [15–20] *II* Isa. 62. 6–end Ps. 97 Titus 3. 4–7 Luke 2. [1–7] 8–20 *III* Isa. 52. 7–10 Ps. 98 Heb. 1. 1–4 [5–12] John 1. 1–14	*MP*: Ps. *110*; 117 Isa. 62. 1–5 Matt. 1. 18–end
	♍			
26	M	STEPHEN, DEACON, FIRST MARTYR	2 Chron. 24. 20–22 *or* Acts 7. 51–end Ps. 119. 161–168 Acts 7. 51–end *or* Gal. 2. 16b–20 Matt. 10. 17–22	*MP*: Ps. *13*; 31. 1–8; 150 Jer. 26. 12–15 Acts ch. 6
	R			
27	Tu	JOHN, APOSTLE AND EVANGELIST	Exod. 33. 7–11a Ps. 117 1 John ch. 1 John 21. 19b–end	*MP*: Ps. *21*; 147. 13–end Exod. 33. 12–end 1 John 2. 1–11
	W			
28	W	THE HOLY INNOCENTS	Jer. 31. 15–17 Ps. 124 1 Cor. 1. 26–29 Matt. 2. 13–18	*MP*: Ps. *36*; 146 Baruch 4. 21–27 *or* Gen. 37. 13–20 Matt. 18. 1–10
	R			
29	Th	**Thomas Becket, Archbishop of Canterbury, Martyr, 1170***		
		Com. Martyr *or* *esp.* Matt. 10. 28–33	1 John 2. 3–11 Ps. 96. 1–4	Ps. *19*; 20 Jonah ch. 1
	Wr	*also* Ecclus. 51. 1–8	Luke 2. 22–35	Col. 1. 1–14
30	F		1 John 2. 12–17 Ps. 96. 7–10	Ps. 111; 112; *113* Jonah ch. 2
	W		Luke 2. 36–40	Col. 1. 15–23
31	Sa	*John Wyclif, Reformer, 1384*	1 John 2. 18–21 Ps. 96. 1, 11–end John 1. 1–18	Ps. 102 Jonah chs 3 & 4 Col. 1.24 – 2.7
	W			

*Thomas Becket may be celebrated on 7 July instead of 29 December.

Second Service Evening Prayer		Calendar and Holy Communion	Morning Prayer	Evening Prayer
EP: Ps. 8 Isa. 65. 17–25 Phil. 2. 5–11 or Luke 2. 1–20 *if it has not been used at the principal service of the day*		**CHRISTMAS DAY** Isa. 9. 2–7 Ps. 98 Heb. 1. 1–12 John 1. 1–14	Ps. *110*; 117 Isa. 62. 1–5 Matt. 1. 18–end	Ps. 8 Isa. 65. 17–25 Phil. 2. 5–11 or Luke 2. 1–20
	𝄌			
EP: Ps. 57; *86* Gen. 4. 1–10 Matt. 23. 34–end	R	STEPHEN, DEACON, FIRST MARTYR Collect (1) Stephen (2) Christmas 2 Chron. 24. 20–22 Ps. 119. 161–168 Acts 7. 55–end Matt. 23. 34–end	(Ps. *13*; 31. 1–8; 150) Jer. 26. 12–15 Acts ch. 6	(Ps. 57; *86*) Gen. 4. 1–10 Matt. 10. 17–22
EP: Ps. 97 Isa. 6. 1–8 1 John 5. 1–12	W	JOHN, APOSTLE AND EVANGELIST Collect (1) John (2) Christmas Exod. 33. 18–end Ps. 92. 11–end 1 John ch. 1 John 21. 19b–end	(Ps. *21*; 147. 13–end) Exod. 33. 7–11a 1 John 2. 1–11	(Ps. 97) Isa. 6. 1–8 1 John 5. 1–12
EP: Ps. 123; *128* Isa. 49. 14–25 Mark 10. 13–16	R	THE HOLY INNOCENTS Collect (1) Innocents (2) Christmas Jer. 31. 10–17 Ps. 123 Rev. 14. 1–5 Matt. 2. 13–18	(Ps. *36*; 146) Baruch 4. 21–27 or Gen. 37. 13–20 Matt. 18. 1–10	(Ps. 124; *128*) Isa. 49. 14–25 Mark 10. 13–16
Ps. 131; *132* Isa. 57. 15–end John 1. 1–18	W		Jonah ch. 1 Col. 1. 1–14	Isa. 57. 15–end John 1. 1–18
Ps. *65*; 84 Isa. 59. 1–15a John 1. 19–28	W		Jonah ch. 2 Col. 1. 15–23	Isa. 59. 1–15a John 1. 19–28
Ps. *90*; 148 Isa. 59. 15b–end John 1. 29–34 *or First EP of The Naming of Jesus* Ps. 148 Jer. 23. 1–6 Col. 2. 8–15 ct	W	Silvester, Bishop of Rome, 335 Com. Bishop	Jonah chs 3 & 4 Col. 1.24 – 2.7	Isa. 59. 15b–end John 1. 29–34 *or First EP of The Circumcision of Christ* (Ps. 148) Jer. 23. 1–6 Col. 2. 8–15 ct

CALENDAR 2011

JANUARY
Su	2 (X²)	9 (B)	16 (E²)	23 (E³)	30 (E⁴)
M	3	10	17	24	31
Tu	4	11	18	25	
W	5	12	19	26	
Th	6 (E)	13	20	27	
F	7	14	21	28	
Sa	1	8	15	22	29

FEBRUARY
Su	6 (L⁻⁴)	13 (L⁻³)	20 (L⁻²)	27 (L⁻¹)	
M	7	14	21	28	
Tu	1	8	15	22	
W	2 (Pr)	9	16	23	
Th	3	10	17	24	
F	4	11	18	25	
Sa	5	12	19	26	

MARCH
Su	6	13 (L¹)	20 (L²)	27 (L³)	
M	7	14	21	28	
Tu	1	8	15	22	29
W	2	9 (A)	16	23	30
Th	3	10	17	24	31
F	4	11	18	25 (An)	
Sa	5	12	19	26	

APRIL
Su	3 (L⁴)	10 (L⁵)	17 (P)	24 (E)	
M	4	11	18	25	
Tu	5	12	19	26	
W	6	13	20	27	
Th	7	14	21 (M)	28	
F	1	8	15	22 (G)	29
Sa	2	9	16	23	30

MAY
Su	1 (E²)	8 (E³)	15 (E⁴)	22 (E⁵)	29 (E⁶)
M	2	9	16	23	30
Tu	3	10	17	24	31
W	4	11	18	25	
Th	5	12	19	26	
F	6	13	20	27	
Sa	7	14	21	28	

JUNE
Su	5	12 (W)	19 (T)	26	
M	6	13	20	27	
Tu	7	14	21	28	
W	1	8	15	22	29
Th	2 (A)	9	16	23	30
F	3	10	17	24	
Sa	4	11	18	25	

JULY
Su	3 (T²)	10 (T³)	17 (T⁴)	24 (T⁵)	31 (T⁶)
M	4	11	18	25	
Tu	5	12	19	26	
W	6	13	20	27	
Th	7	14	21	28	
F	1	8	15	22	29
Sa	2	9	16	23	30

AUGUST
Su	7 (T⁷)	14 (T⁸)	21 (T⁹)	28 (T¹⁰)	
M	1	8	15	22	29
Tu	2	9	16	23	30
W	3	10	17	24	31
Th	4	11	18	25	
F	5	12	19	26	
Sa	6	13	20	27	

SEPTEMBER
Su	4 (T¹¹)	11 (T¹²)	18 (T¹³)	25 (T¹⁴)	
M	5	12	19	26	
Tu	6	13	20	27	
W	7	14	21	28	
Th	1	8	15	22	29
F	2	9	16	23	30
Sa	3	10	17	24	

OCTOBER
Su	2 (T¹⁵)	9 (T¹⁶)	16 (T¹⁷)	23 (T¹⁸)	30 (T¹⁹)
M	3	10	17	24	31
Tu	4	11	18	25	
W	5	12	19	26	
Th	6	13	20	27	
F	7	14	21	28	
Sa	1	8	15	22	29

NOVEMBER
Su	6 (A⁻³)	13 (A⁻²)	20 (A⁻¹)	27 (A¹)	
M	7	14	21	28	
Tu	1 (AS)	8	15	22	29
W	2	9	16	23	30
Th	3	10	17	24	
F	4	11	18	25	
Sa	5	12	19	26	

DECEMBER
Su	4 (A²)	11 (A³)	18 (A⁴)	25 (X)	
M	5	12	19	26	
Tu	6	13	20	27	
W	7	14	21	28	
Th	1	8	15	22	29
F	2	9	16	23	30
Sa	3	10	17	24	31

Legend (Calendar 2011)

- A = Ash Wednesday, Ascension, Advent
- A⁻ = Before Advent
- A⁻¹ = also All Saints (if transferred)
- A⁻¹ = Christ the King
- An = Annunciation
- AS = All Saints
- B = Baptism
- E = Epiphany, Easter
- E⁴ = also Presentation (if transferred)
- G = Good Friday
- L = Lent
- L⁻ = Before Lent

CALENDAR 2012

JANUARY
Su	1 (X¹)	8 (E²)	15 (E³)	22 (E⁴)	29 (E⁵)
M	2	9	16	23	30
Tu	3	10	17	24	31
W	4	11	18	25	
Th	5	12	19	26	
F	6 (E)	13	20	27	
Sa	7	14	21	28	

FEBRUARY
Su	5 (L⁻³)	12 (L⁻²)	19 (L⁻¹)	26 (L¹)	
M	6	13	20	27	
Tu	7	14	21	28	
W	1	8	15	22 (A)	29
Th	2 (Pr)	9	16	23	
F	3	10	17	24	
Sa	4	11	18	25	

MARCH
Su	4 (L²)	11 (L³)	18 (L⁴)	25 (L⁵)	
M	5	12	19	26	
Tu	6	13	20	27	
W	7	14	21	28	
Th	1	8	15	22	29
F	2	9	16	23	30
Sa	3	10	17	24	31 (An)

APRIL
Su	1 (P)	8 (E)	15 (E²)	22 (E³)	29 (E⁴)
M	2	9	16	23	30
Tu	3	10	17	24	
W	4	11	18	25	
Th	5 (M)	12	19	26	
F	6 (G)	13	20	27	
Sa	7	14	21	28	

MAY
Su	6 (E⁵)	13 (E⁶)	20 (E⁷)	27 (W)	
M	7	14	21	28	
Tu	1	8	15	22	29
W	2	9	16	23	30
Th	3	10	17 (A)	24	31
F	4	11	18	25	
Sa	5	12	19	26	

JUNE
Su	3 (T)	10	17	24 (T⁵)	
M	4	11	18	25	
Tu	5	12	19	26	
W	6	13	20	27	
Th	7	14	21	28	
F	1	8	15	22	29
Sa	2	9	16	23	30

JULY
Su	1 (T⁵)	8	15	22 (T⁷)	29
M	2	9	16	23	30
Tu	3	10	17	24	31
W	4	11	18	25	
Th	5	12	19	26	
F	6	13	20	27	
Sa	7	14	21	28	

AUGUST
Su	5 (T⁹)	12 (T¹⁰)	19	26 (T¹²)	
M	6	13	20	27	
Tu	7	14	21	28	
W	1	8	15	22	29
Th	2	9	16	23	30
F	3	10	17	24	31
Sa	4	11	18	25	

SEPTEMBER
Su	2 (T¹³)	9 (T¹⁴)	16 (T¹⁵)	23 (T¹⁶)	30 (T¹⁷)
M	3	10	17	24	
Tu	4	11	18	25	
W	5	12	19	26	
Th	6	13	20	27	
F	7	14	21	28	
Sa	1	8	15	22	29

OCTOBER
Su	7 (T¹⁸)	14 (T¹⁹)	21 (T²⁰)	28	
M	1	8	15	22	29
Tu	2	9	16	23	30
W	3	10	17	24	31
Th	4	11	18	25	
F	5	12	19	26	
Sa	6	13	20	27	

NOVEMBER
Su	4 (A⁻³)	11 (A⁻²)	18 (A⁻¹)	25 (A¹)	
M	5	12	19	26	
Tu	6	13	20	27	
W	7	14	21	28	
Th	1 (AS)	8	15	22	29
F	2	9	16	23	30
Sa	3	10	17	24	

DECEMBER
Su	2 (A²)	9 (A³)	16 (A⁴)	23 (A⁵)	30 (X¹)
M	3	10	17	24	31
Tu	4	11	18	25 (X)	
W	5	12	19	26	
Th	6	13	20	27	
F	7	14	21	28	
Sa	1	8	15	22	29

Legend (Calendar 2012)

- M = Maundy Thursday
- P = Palm Sunday
- Pr = Presentation
- T = Trinity
- (T²) = also Thomas, 2011)
- (T³) = also Simon and Jude, 2012)
- (T⁵) = also Birth of John the Baptist, 2012)
- (T⁷) = also Mary Magdalene, 2012)
- T⁻ = Last Sunday after Trinity
- W = Pentecost (Whit Sunday)
- X = Christmas